Papier-mache
KING GOTHIC TRAY
19th century

An
ILLUSTRATED GLOSSARY
of
DECORATED ANTIQUES

From the Late 17th Century
To the Early 20th Century

by MARYJANE CLARK

A Publication of
THE HISTORICAL SOCIETY
of
EARLY AMERICAN DECORATION, INC.

CHARLES E. TUTTLE COMPANY: PUBLISHERS
Rutland, Vermont

REPRESENTATIVES

Continental Europe: Boxerbooks, Inc., Zurich

British Isles: Prentice-Hall International, Inc., London

Australasia: Paul Flesch & Co., Pty. Ltd., Melbourne

Canada: M. G. Hurtig Ltd., Edmonton

Published by the Charles E. Tuttle Company, Inc.

of Rutland, Vermont & Tokyo, Japan

with editorial offices at

2-6, Suido 1-chome, Tokyo, Japan (112)

Library of congress catalog card number   74-138080

International standard book number 0-8048-0953-4

Printed in Japan

CONTENTS

ACKNOWLEDGMENTS

My first acknowledgment goes to Mrs. Sherwood Martin
whose idea it was to set this book in motion, then to
the Historical Society of Early American Decoration.
whose trustees accepted it as their fourth publication.
This could not have been done without the experience
of Mrs. Adrian M. Lea, Publications Chairman, and Mrs.
Catherine Hutter, who copy-edited the book for me.

To cover all types of ornamented pieces of wood, leather, tin, paper-mâché, glass, or metal would be practically impossible, but I have tried to include the most
characteristic examples.

I deeply appreciate the contribution of Mrs. Frederick
Baker and Mrs. Fred Lightbourn on Chests; of Mrs. Ly-
man Mears on Cornice Boards; of Mrs. Edwin Rowell and
Mrs. D. F. Heatherington on Looking Glasses. Mrs.
Charles Tanner and Mrs. Vernon Hall assisted with the
material on Clocks; the Bellows sequence was checked by
Mrs. Harry MacDuffie. A fruitful visit with Mr. John
T. Kenney, president of the Hitchcock Chair Company,
put the Hitchcock chairs in their proper order. I am
most grateful to him. Mrs. Max Muller and Mrs. Sylves-
ter Poor gave information on New York and Maine tin.
The many hours spent by Mrs. Edwin Rowell on historical
information notes are highly appreciated. Technical
help came from Mrs. R. Litchfield, Mrs. C. Gearin, Mrs.
J. Phelps and Miss Helen Lincoln; originals to be re-
produced from Mrs. Sherwood Martin, Mrs. George DeVoe,
Mrs. Gordon S. Kipp, Mrs. William R. Carter, Mrs. John
Clinkman, Mrs. W. W. Stainton, Mrs. Philip Wheelock,
Mr. and Mrs. Robert Keegan, and others.

My profoundest thanks to Mrs. Frost Walker, Mrs. J.
Stevens and Mrs. T. Carlsen for helping me with the
illustrations, and to Mr. Barry Wood for reducing them
photographically; to Mrs. Philip Wheelock for her com-
petent assistance with the vocabulary, and to Mrs. Eu-

gene Bond for the many hours she spent checking the
material in the glossary.

To the following organizations I wish to add my thanks
for their available material: Winterthur Museum, Winterthur, Delaware; Philadelphia Museum of Art, Philadelphia, Pennsylvania; New York State Historical Association, Cooperstown, New York; Cooper Hewitt Museum,
New York City; Historical Society of Early American Decoration, Inc. Headquarters at Cooperstown; Old Sturbridge Village, Sturbridge, Massachusetts; Hershey Estates Museum, Hershey, Pennsylvania; Museum of Fine
Arts, Boston, Massachusetts; Victoria and Albert Museum,
London, England; Peabody Museum, Salem, Massachusetts;
Connecticut Historical Society, Hartford, Connecticut;
Metropolitan Museum of Art, New York, New York; and National Museum of Wales, Cardiff.

All these generously contributed efforts, and the many
visits with Mrs. George DeVoe and Mrs. Sherwood Martin
will show, I hope, in the eventual success of this book.

                                        Maryjane Clark
Scrabble Arts
Norwell, Mass.

FOREWORD
by
JESSICA BOND

A debt of gratitude is due to the author of this first
book on the terminology used in the decoration of antiques abroad and in the United States in the eighteenth
and nineteenth centuries. It was fitting that the need
for this book be fulfilled by one who has spent over
thirty years recording decorated objects, instructing
and collecting in the wide field of what has come to be
known as "Early American Decoration."

Mrs. Clark, a master craftsman and master teacher of the
Historical Society of Early American Decoration, recognized -- with others -- the need to develop a common
language among collectors, dealers, and decorators, and
has spent the past five years compiling this glossary
and making the intricate drawings which add so much to
the written description. It has been written under the
auspices of the Historical Society of Early American Decoration which was founded in 1946 by the students of
the late Esther Stevens Brazer, well-known author of
Early American Decoration, a comprehensive book on that
subject, which was published in 1941 and is now in its
fourth printing. In the span of twenty-three years or
more, the over seven hundred members of this organiza-
tion have gone far in the study of ornament as used in
the homes of our forefathers.

Some items were brought here by the colonists; others
were imported later;, some were made and decorated in the
United States; others were manufactured abroad. All are
of historic interest. Decorated furniture, cornice
boards, tin trunks, teapots, trays, bellows, glass tablets for clocks and looking glasses, as well as painted
and stenciled walls and floors are a few examples of
the early craftsmen's work which came under the scrutiny
of Early American Decoration. The date an article was

made and decorated; the regional characteristics of the
designs -- Is it painted or stenciled? Is it worked in
gold leaf or freehand bronze? Is the decoration original with the article? These are the problems of the
researcher.

To the layman, to employ the words "stencil," "tole,"
or "gold leaf" may sound meaningful; actually he may
be using the incorrect term. The terms used in this
book are those used among researchers, craftsmen, students, and teachers in the field of antique ornamented
wares. It should prove beneficial to dealers who sell
these wares, and to museums that display and catalogue
them, and appreciate their importance as part of the
history of ornamentation in the American home.

About
ESTHER STEVENS BRAZER
by
BETH DOBLE

No publication of the Historical Society of Early American Decoration would be complete without mention of
Esther Stevens Brazer, whose tireless research and
teaching are the foundation on which the Society rests
today. We are therefore grateful to her friend and
colleague, Beth Doble, for this brief account of her
life.

Esther Stevens Brazer was born in Portland, Maine, in
1898. At the age of ten her mother died quite suddenly and Esther developed a baffling illness that kept
her in bed much of the time. She had a special teacher
in design, composition, and color. She was a preco-
cious child.

In her early teens she read books on archeology, Greek
mythology, crafts of the American Indian; she also had
an insatiable interest in constructing things. She
made herself a toy theatre with dolls in Grecian robes,
as on the Greek vases.

In high school she chose the boys' course and was the
only girl among forty boys in the class. After finishing her college preparatory course she took a year's
training at Portland Art School, then she enrolled as
a special student at Columbia University. There she
found that a fine interior decorating course for senior
students was scheduled. She overcame all objections
and entered the course.

War broke out and she switched to a course in statistics
for war service which brought her to a post as statisti-

cian on the Shipping Board. Several years later, after
recovering from a serious illness, she realized that
she had to alter her way of life, and so turned to art
work again. Suddenly, while cleaning off an old chair,
a stenciled design appeared, but she didn't know the
technique to reproduce it. She tried every device with
no success. While visiting home in Portland she went
to see several collectors who had stenciled chairs.
One of the collectors remarked, "If you <u>really</u> want to
know about stenciling, go see Geórge Lord."

She found Mr. Lord painting, in spite of the fact that
he was eighty-seven years old and deaf. Mrs. Brazer
said he must have sensed that he might not be decorating
much longer and that he would do well to show the tricks
of his trade to someone whose interest was as keen as
his. He varnished a piece of black paper, reached up
on a high shelf for his folders and stencils marked
"flowers, leaves, and scrolls," then opened a cigar box
in which he kept his bronze powders in partitions. She
watched him work for about fifteen minutes, during
which he revealed to her the whole process of stenciling.
"If I had had longer to work, there were lots of freehand
tricks he could have shown me," she said.

As her interest in stenciled designs increased, she realized there were many other patterns that could be worked
out by freehand methods. She met the editor of <u>An-
tiques Magazine</u>, the late Homer Eaton Keyes. He encouraged her to pursue her studies. Thus she became a pioneer in antique painted design, a mechanically lost art.
Through Mr. Keyes she met her husband, an architect, Dr.
Clarence Brazer, who, realizing that she had much to
give, encouraged her to teach and write her book, <u>Early
American Decoration</u>, published in 1940 and now in its
fourth printing.

In 1945 she died. Her students, wishing to continue the
research she had begun, formed a guild called the Esther
Stevens Brazer Guild, which was given a charter in 1950
and is known today as the Historical Society of Early
American Decoration, Inc., with its headquarters and mu-

seum in Cooperstown, New York. In this glossary the
Society's name, wherever used, has been abbreviated to
HSEAD.

About the Author
MARYJANE CLARK

MARYJANE CLARK is one of the finest craftsmen, researchers and teachers in the Historical Society of Early
American Decoration. She was a member, in 1948, before
it became a Historical Society, of the Esther Stevens
Brazer Guild. In 1955 she became a Master Craftsman,
and in 1960 a Master Teacher, which authorizes her to
practice and teach the Society's various craft techniques: stenciling, country painting, gold leaf and
freehand bronze work, painting and gold leaf etching on
glass, so-called "lace edge" painting and Chippendale
painting. She has taught in Massachusetts in the public
schools of Hansen, Hanover and Cohasset, and is present-
ly teaching at her studio, Scrabble Arts, in Norwell,
Massachusetts.

Since her graduation in 1936 from the Amy Sacker School
of Design in Boston, she has been actively engaged in
teaching, research, lecturing, writing, decorating, re-
storing and exhibiting. She has done extensive research
on early American decoration and its European origins
not only in the United States but also in Europe. Maryjane Clark has been chairman of the Society's Teacher's
Certification Committee and is at present chairman of
the Standards and Judging Committee, which is responsible for the high quality of craftsmanship that the
Society is ever anxious to maintain. She is a member
of Sturbridge Village, Massachusetts, of the Connecticut
Historical Society, of the Board of Directors of the
Norwell Historical Society and past Treasurer and President of the Norwell Art Association. Years of research
and artistic endeavor went into the compilation of this
Glossary.

How to Use
THE GLOSSARY

The inked line illustrations have been sketched from
pictures, photographs, slides, and original pieces. In
each case a description of the decoration has been included, since the type of design and technique used often date a piece. Unless the article was signed and/or
dated, the dates given are approximate. As much as
possible, the place of origin is listed, although we
realize that decorators moved from shop to shop and
ideas were copied.

In attempting to identify an unknown piece, it is sug-
gested that the Table of Contents be checked first for
the proper category. If the reader is in doubt as to
the category, the Index will provide a second check of
the information available. The vocabulary includes
mainly terms of a descriptive nature pertaining to the
various articles described in the Glossary.

Categories have been limited to one or two illustrations
of representative types, and the articles have been arranged in alphabetical sequence within the categories
themselves. The captions try to provide the reader with
as much historical information as possible; where more
explicit data is required, it may be found under the
headings "Design," "Painters and Craftsmen," "Inventors
and Inventions," "Tinsmiths and Tin Centers," "Manufacturers and Manufactories," which include information
relevant to articles in the Glossary only. No attempt
has been made to list all known decorators, inventors,
manufacturers, etc., since we felt this would have gone
beyond the immediate purposes and limits of this book.

We hope that laymen, dealers in antiques, and craftsmen
will become more knowledgeable of the historical background in the field of ornamentation and more familiar
with the correct terms and techniques, thanks to this
volume.

ACCESSORIES
in
GLASS

REVERSE GOLD LEAF ON GLASS

PICTURE, reverse gold leaf. Very finely engraved.
Signed: G. Geiser, 1887. Possibly New York.   Fig.1

TINSEL PICTURE. New England, 1825-
1875. 10" x 12". The design outlined in ink on the reverse side of
the glass. The flowers are washed
with tinsel. The backgrounds beyond the designs were white, cream,
or black. This one is black.

Fig.2

TINSEL PICTURES

Oriental, crystal, or tinsel painting reached its peak
in 1866. Transparent oil painting was done, in reverse,
on glass, then embellished with a tin foil or pearl
shell backing.

TINSEL PICTURE. Bird on nest, butterfly, flowers, and
leaves. Cream background.   Fig.3

ACCESSORIES
in
LEATHER

FIRE BUCKETS

These were done by two early artisans, the shoemaker
and the glazier, who lettered and painted a name, number,
or design on the hand-sewn tanned leather bucket. They
were tight in spite of being hand-sewn, and were much
used. Coat-of-arms, eagles, hands clasped in friend-
ship were some of the motifs that identify the bucket.
1794-1850.

FIRE BUCKET. American. 1810. Eagle motif, painted in oil.   Fig.4

FIRE BUCKET. New York. Circa 1845.
Eagle and scroll painted yellow,
brown, and green. Approximately 12"
x 7".   Fig.5

GUNPOWDER CARRIER. Connecticut.
1775-1783. 26" high, 9 1/2" diameter. A gold-leaf and painted design.   Fig.6

<u>DRUM</u> of the 9th Regiment, Vermont Volunteers, U. S. In-
fantry. Circa 1860. Painted. Red frame top and bottom,
deep blue background behind yellow ochre eagle. Fig.7

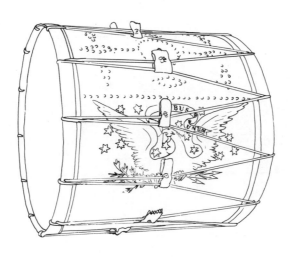

<u>SMALL BASS DRUM.</u>   Circa 1775.   Painted on leather. Fig.8

ACCESSORIES
in
METAL

BANKS

Sometimes called "still banks" (because they have no
moving parts?). Imported and sold by Hull & Stafford
and Goodrich, Ives & Co. 1850-1870. 4" x 2 1/4" x
1 1/4" or larger. The design is stenciled on backgrounds of black asphaltum, clear brown, green, blue,
opaque red, and yellow.

Fig.9A   Fig.9B   Fig.9C   Fig.9D

GOTHIC BANK   COTTAGE BANK   HOUSE BANK
Fig.9E   Fig.9F   Fig.9G

BASKETS

Apple, bread, bun, sometimes called "trays."

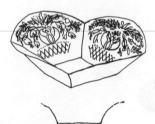

APPLE BASKET. American. Circa
1840. 12" wide, 2 1/2" high, 4"
square floor. Made mostly in
Connecticut. Stenciled, with
color washes, on a black ground.
Fig.10

APPLE BASKET.   Made in New England,
New York, New Jersey, and Pennsylvania. From 1840. Many sizes,
from miniature to 15" across. This
one is 10 1/2" x 2 1/2", with 5"
square floor. The backgrounds are
black, white, asphaltum, or colored, with country-painting designs.
                                Fig.11

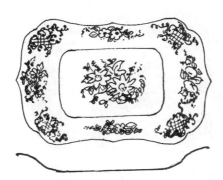

BREAD BASKET. Gothic shape. Midlands, England. Circa 1860. 11 1/2" x 9 3/4" x 2 1/4" deep. Gold-leaf
and freehand bronzing on a deep red, grained background.   Fig.12

BREAD BASKET. England. Circa 1810. 8 1/2" x 15 1/2"
x 2 1/4". Flower painting with freehand bronze and gold
leaf on a black background.   Fig.13

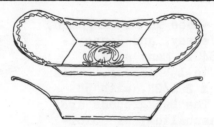

BREAD BASKET. New York. 1826. 13 1/4" x 7" x 2 3/4"
at the ends, and 1 1/8" at the center. The design is
typical country painting from the Butler shop. Fig.14

BREAD BASKET. Wolverhampton, England. Circa 1810.
12 1/2" x 10" x 1 1/2". The narrow sandwich edge is
decorated with a gold leaf design. The floor is painted with flowers, today called "Chippendale" painting.
Black background.   Fig.15

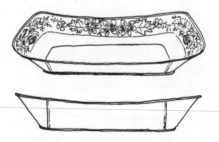

BREAD BASKET. England, Midlands. Circa 1850. 14 3/4"
x 2 7/8" and 2" deep in the center. Oblong basket
stenciled on a black background.   Fig.16

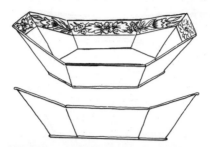

BUN BASKET. England, Midlands. Circa 1849. 8" x
15" x 3 3/4" and 2 3/4" at the center. Octagonal.
Negative stenciling on a black background.   Fig.17

BUN BASKET. New York. Circa 1830. 8 1/2" x 12 3/4"
x 4 1/2". Country painting, typical of Ann Butler. A
boat-shaped basket with hand holes.   Fig.18

BUN BASKET. Pontypool, Wales. 1790-1820. 13" x
7 1/2" x 2". Oval, with hand holes and pierced flange.
"Lace-edge" painting on a black background.   Fig.19

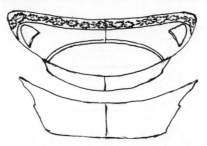

<u>BUN BASKET</u>. England. Circa 1800. 8 1/4" x 14" x 4".
The floor is 6 1/4" x 10 1/2". Oval or boat-shaped,
with handholes. Gold-leaf border design on the flange.
                                                        Fig.20

<u>BUN BASKET</u>. American, Maine. Circa 1830. 7 1/2" x
13" x 2 1/2" at ends; 2" at center. Oval, with hand
holes and pierced flange. Wet-on-wet painting on a
black background, which is typical of Maine.   Fig.21

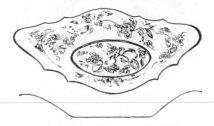

<u>BUN BASKET</u>. Victorian shape. England. Circa 1840.
12" x 9 1/2" x 1 3/4". 1 1/2" at center. Design:
flowers and gold-leaf sprays. Today called "Chippendale" painting.   Fig.22

<u>BUN BASKET</u>. Connecticut. Circa 1830. 11" x 6 1/2" x
2" at center. Oval or boat-shaped, with hand holes.
Country painting in red, green, and yellow. Note the
border on the outside.   Fig.23

<u>BUN BASKET</u>, miniature. From the
Filley Shop, New York. 1815-1825.
6 1/2" x 4 1/2" x 2"; 1 1/2" at
center. The floor is 3" x 4 3/4".
Country painting in red, green,
and yellow.   Fig.24

<u>LACE-EDGE PAINTED, PIERCED-EDGE BASKETS</u>

The name of this style of painting and the type of article on which it was used originated probably with Esther Stevens Brazer, and was inspired by the lacy effect
of the pierced edge of such wares.

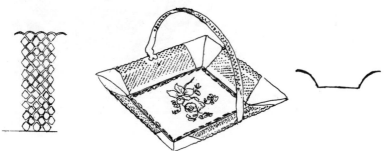

<u>PIERCED-EDGE BASKET</u>, with swinging handle. Pontypool,
Wales. Circa 1780. 6 1/2" x 6 1/2" x 1 3/4". Overlapped joints at the corners. The background is tortoise-shell, with "lace edge" painting and a gold-leaf
border and stripe on the floor. See also p.30. Fig.25

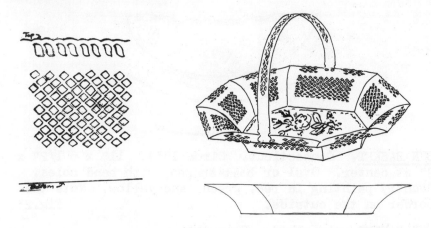

PIERCED-EDGE BASKET. Pontypool, Wales. Circa 1775.
6 1/4" square, 2" tall. Octagonal. "Lace-edge"
painting on a tortoise-shell background.   Fig.26

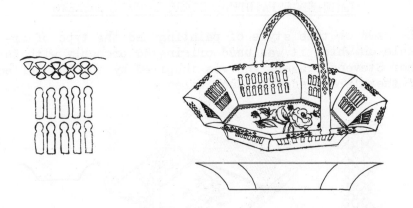

PIERCED-EDGE BASKET. Pontypool, Wales. Circa 1780.
10 1/4" overall; floor 6 1/4". 1 3/4" tall. Pierced
rim and handle. Two rows of keyhole piercing. "Lace-
edge" painting on a tortoise-shell background. Fig.27

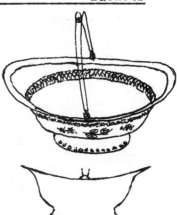

PIERCED-EDGE BASKET. England.
1810.   13 3/4" x 5" x 3.1/4", with
a 1/2" sandwich-edge rim. "Lace-
edge" painting and gold-leaf border.
Fig.28

PIERCED-EDGE BASKET. France. Circa
1820. 15" x 9 1/4" x 2". Green
and umber scrolls on a yellow background. Note the interesting
piercing. Some of the French pieces
tend to be heavier than others.
Fig.29

PIERCED-EDGE BASKET. France.
1860's. A yellow background with
painted strokes at the ends and
bronze stripes.   Fig.30

SWEETMEAT BASKET. Pontypool,
Wales. Circa 1770. 7" x 2 7/8".
Pierced flat rim and handle. Gold
leaf on a black japanned background.
Fig.31

BOTTLE STANDS, see WINE COASTERS

BOWLS

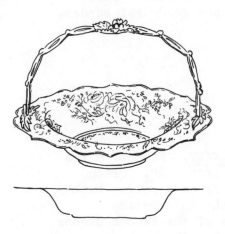

GOTHIC BOWL, with brass handles. Midlands, England.
1840-1850. 8 1/4" x 1 1/4". Gold-leaf border and so-
called "Chippendale" painting from rim to floor.
Sandwich edge.   Fig.32

OVAL BOWL. Bilston, England. After 1850. 13 1/2" x
10 3/4". Rim rolled over wire. A one-piece stencil on
the floor. The design on the border is stamped with a
cork. Color washes over the fruit. Red background on
top, black on bottom. This may have been a Bilston blank
and decorated elsewhere.   Fig.33

SERVING BOWL. England. Circa 1865. Red and black
background with a fine gold-leaf design.   Fig.34

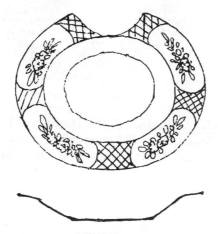

SHAVING BOWL or basin. Also called a "barbers' bleed-
ing bowl." Pontypool, Wales. 1790. 11 1/2" x 2 1/2".
Fine gold leaf design on a mottled red background, similar to tortoise-shell.   Fig.35

SUGAR BOWL. Holland. Hallmarked
before 1750. Pewter, hexagonal
shape. 3 3/4" tall, 7 1/2" across.
Was evidently decorated by a fine
Pontypool painter. Lace-edge
painting and gold-leaf borders. A
reddish glow coming through the
background gives the tortoise-shell
effect so typical of Pontypool work.
Hallmarks on the bowl are shown at
the right.   Fig.36

SUGAR BOWL. Connecticut. Circa
1820. 4 1/4" x 3 1/2". Lightly
flaired footing; rolled under bottom, which is not wired; hand-roll-
ed topknot. Country painting on a
dark asphaltum background. Fig.37

VICTORIAN BOWL. England, Midlands. 1840-1850. 15" x
12" x 3". So-called "Chippendale" painting on a blue
background. Also found on green and black.   Fig.38

BOXES

Fig.39A

Fig.39B

BIBLE BOXES. Sometimes called "prayer book" or "book"
boxes. Fig. 39A: 3 1/4" x 2 1/2" x 1", yellow background. Fig.39B: 5 3/4" x 3 3/4" x 1 1/8", green background. Maine pieces, both with country painting. Fig.39

CANDLE BOX. New England. 1880.
13 1/2" x 4". The design is stenciled on an asphaltum background.
Also found with country-painted designs.   Fig.40

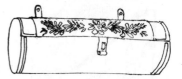

DEED OR DOCUMENT BOXES, see TRUNKS

GIFT OR TRINKET BOX. Maine. 1798-
1830. 10" x 10" x 4 1/2". The
country painting by Z. Stevens.
                          Fig.41

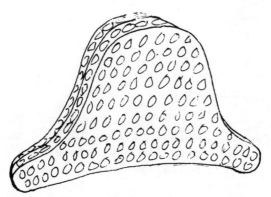

HAT BOX, tricornered. England. 1830-1840. 19 1/2"
long, 8 1/4" high, 4" deep, with thumb-print design in
a dark asphaltum background. Handle in the middle of
the bottom.   Fig.42

KNIFE BOX. Pontypool, Wales.
Circa 1760. 9 1/2" x 9 1/2" x
16 1/2" high. Gold-leaf chinoiserie on a tortoise-shell background.
Bottom edge pierced, resting on
ball feet. Brass handle and lock.
                                Fig.43

KNIFE BOX. Pontypool, Wales. 1755-
1760. 9 1/2" x 16 1/2" by 9 1/2"
deep. Lace-edge painting and embossed gold borders. Pierced bottom
on ball feet.   Fig.44

KNIFE BOX. Urn shape. Pontypool,
Wales. 1740. 16 1/2" tall. Brunswick blacked, silver stripes with an
alizarian wash. Fine early piece.
                                Fig.45

NUTMEG BOX. English. 1800's. 2" x
1" wide and 1" deep. Asphaltum background with a gold bronze stripe and
flower design. Lift the lid, and it
has a small grater. This type box
was carried in the vest pocket and
used to grate fresh nutmeg into one's
drink.   Fig.46

NUTMEG BOX. Connecticut. Mid-19th
century. 4" x 2 3/4" x 2 1/4".
Transparent blue background. Stenciling in two tones of bronze, with yellow brush strokes on the hasp.
                               Fig.47

OVAL BOX. American. Early 1800's.
Country painting. Sometimes used
for collars.   Fig.48

OVAL DOME-TOP BOX. Pennsylvania.
1820-1850. 10" x 8 3/4". In five
graduated sizes. Used for flour,
sugar, and other dry ingredients.
The gay design is country painting
on a red background.   Fig.49

PINCUSHION BOX. Maine. 1798-1830.
Octagonal gift box done in Maine
country-painting style by Z. Stevens.
                                    Fig.50

RECTANGULAR BOX. Also called a BIS-
CUIT BOX. England, Midlands. Circa
1850. So-called "Chippendale" painting and gold-leaf scrolls on a black
background. 6" long, 3 1/4" deep,
4 1/2" high.   Fig.51

SNUFF BOX. Pontypool, Wales. Circa
1850. 3 1/4" x 2 1/4" x 1". It
came in various shapes and was found
inscribed with many sayings such as
"Here's Health to our Sick," in gilt,
with a gilt scroll on a black asphaltum background.   Fig.52

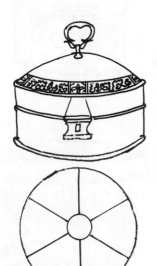

SPICE BOX. Usk, Wales. 1840. 7"
in diameter, 6 1/4" tall, with a dome
top, brass handle, and attractive
English hasp. Inside are six spice
sections, grater in the center. Gold
leaf border on black asphaltum background.   Fig.53

Inside view.   Fig.53A

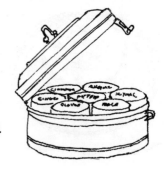

SPICE BOX. Boston, Massachusetts.
Circa 1871. 7" in diameter, 4 1/4"
high. Stamped-out top. Stenciled
spice names on spice boxes, on an
asphaltum ground. Bronze stripes.
                                    Fig.54

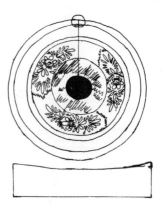

SPIT BOX. Later called a SPITTOON.
Connecticut. Circa 1860. 8" x
2 1/4". White smoked background
with a transparent blue background
under the negative stencil.   Fig.55

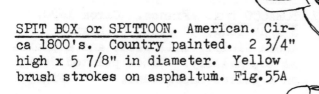

SPIT BOX or SPITTOON. American. Circa 1800's. Country painted. 2 3/4"
high x 5 7/8" in diameter. Yellow
brush strokes on asphaltum. Fig.55A

TOBACCO BOX. In one piece. Pontypool, Wales. 1775-1785. 4 5/8" a-
cross, 2 3/8" deep. The bottom is
9 1/4" in diameter. Design: polychrome lace-edge painting.   Fig.56

TOBACCO BOX. Pontypool, Wales. Miscalled a "tea box." Circa 1790. 6"
x 4 1/4" x 6 1/4". Ball feet and
flame finial. Freehand bronze and
painted woodland scene. Probably a
copy of Thomas Barker's work, who
painted such scenes. See also Fig.
260.   Fig.57

TOBACCO BOX. France. Circa 1820.
6 1/4" long, 5" wide, 5" high.
Acorn finial, ball feet, and a pierced top gallery. Umber painted design
on a yellow background.   Fig.58

TOBACCO BOX. German. After 1800. Black ground with design in silver and gold. 5 3/4" high; 5" in diameter at base.   Fig.59

TEA CADDIES

TEA CADDY or BOX. Birmingham, England. Circa 1860. 5 1/4" x 5 1/2" x 2 3/4" high. Gothic shape with geometrical design in thick red, blue, and white paint, outlined in metal leaf. Black background. Stamped shape.   Fig.60

TEA CADDY or BOX. Midlands, England. Circa 1870. 5 1/2"
tall. Printed tin. One of many English exports. Gold
colored box, polychrome painting. A small section in
back holds the tea shovel.   Fig.61

TEA CADDY. Midlands, England.
Circa 1830. 4 1/2" x 3 3/8" x 4 1/2"
high. Gothic-shape top. Geometric
design on a white, circular base.
Background mauve and yellow graining
over "shiny" or new tin.   Fig.62

TEA CADDY. Wolverhampton, England.
Circa 1818. 5" long, 4" wide, 5 1/4"
high. Black background. Freehand
bronze design on dusted bronze. Colored washes and painted details.
                              Fig.63

TEA CADDY. New York. Circa 1824.
5" wide x 4" deep x 4 1/2" high.
Knob, lock, and claw feet. Top decorated with white bands and country
painting. Body of caddy, dark asphaltum. Design: red, yellow, blue,
and green. Signed: Ann Butler. Possibly painted on an English piece.
                              Fig.64

TEA CADDY. England. Circa 1840.
Molded top, brass feet and handle.
The design is made up of many stencils on a black ground, each side
different, as in a sample piece;
crisply done. 10" long, 4" wide,
6" high.   Fig.65

TEA CADDY. England. 1840-1860.
5 3/8" long x 4 1/8" wide x 3" high.
Gothic-shaped box has gold leaf,
freehand bronze and impasto (raised)
painting in white on a black background.   Fig.66

CAKE CLOSET. New England. 1870. 11" x 8 1/2" x
16 1/2". Two shelves and four claw feet. A bronzed
pattern with red, green, and white random strokes
constitute the design.   Fig.67

CANDLE ACCESSORIES

CANDELABRUM. Usk, Wales. 1790. 15" high, 18" wide.
Gold-leaf borders on a black background.   Fig.68

CANDLE HOLDER. With a straddle
snuffers section. Birmingham, England. Circa 1820. 7" x 3 1/4" x 4".
The flange and floor have a narrow
gilt border design.   Fig.69

CANDLE HOLDER. American. 1834. 5"
x 2". Country painting, Pennsylvania-
type, with yellow brush strokes on
the flange. Painted leaves and fruit
on a white band on the floor. Fig.70

CHAMBER CANDLE HOLDER. Usk, Wales.
Circa 1778. 4" x 4" x 3". A favorite Usk motif: silver stars on a
black ground. Note hanging extinguisher.   Fig.71

FLATBACK CANDLE HOLDER or SCONCE.
American. 1815-1846. This is when
the crimping machine was introduced
and with it the word "sconce."
9 1/2" x 3". The design is red,
yellow, and green. Country-painting brush strokes on a black background.   Fig.72

CANDLE SNUFFERS ON TRAY. Usk, Wales.
Circa 1778. Stars on a black background, with gilt knobs on the top.
Also called "extinguishers" or "dou-
ters." Made in the Midlands. Fig.73

CANDLE SNUFFER. American. 1830's.
3" x 1 1/4". Yellow and red brush
strokes painted on black asphaltum.
No top knob.   Fig.74

CANDLESTICK. Vase-shaped. Pontypool, Wales. Circa 1770. 10 3/4"
tall on a 3" base. Delicate gold-
leaf painting on a tortoise-shell
background. Some were pewter.
                                  Fig.75

CANDLESTICK. Connecticut. Circa 1824. 5 1/4" tall on a 4 1/4" x 4" base. Yellow brush strokes on asphaltum background.   Fig.76

CANDLESTICK. Square base. England. 1765. 11 1/4" tall on a 3 1/2" base. Flower painting and gold leaf on a deep brown background.   Fig.77

CANDLESTICK. Vase-shaped. Usk, Wales. 1820. Gold leaf border on a black background.   Fig.78

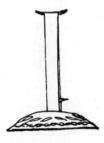

SLIP-UP CANDLESTICK (so-called). American. 1832. 5 1/4" on a 4 1/4" x 4" base. Black background, country painting. Borders of yellow and green strokes.   Fig.79

CANISTERS

COFFEE CANISTER. With steeple top.
Massachusetts. Circa 1871. Possibly made by the Dover Stamping Company. Stenciled design on an asphaltum ground.   Fig.80

GUNPOWDER CANISTER. Flask-shaped.
Connecticut. Circa 1820. 3" wide,
4 1/4" high, and 1 1/2" deep. A
country-painting brushstroke design
on an asphaltum background. Early
canisters had painted designs.Fig.81

GUNPOWDER CANISTER, or SPORTING POW-
DER CANISTER. Connecticut. 1835.
3 1/2" wide, 4 1/4" high, and 1 1/2"
deep. Stenciled design on an asphaltum background.   Fig.82

GUNPOWDER CANISTER, or SPORTING POW-
DER CANISTER. Connecticut. 1835.
3 1/4" wide, 4 1/4" high, and 1 1/4"
deep. Screw top. Made of white
metal, design stenciled on asphaltum.   Fig.83

ROUND CANISTER. Also called a SUGAR
BOX. American. 1800's. These canisters were used for flour or sugar.
Some were decorated with country-
painting designs; some were stenciled.
                                   Fig.84

TEA CANISTER. Octagonal. Possibly decorated in England. Found in New York and Vermont. Circa 1825. 4 1/2" x 3 1/4" x 6 1/2". Design: red, blue-green, and white impasto painting, similar to lace edge.
Fig.85

TEA CANISTER. Oval, with flat top. Probably a New England import. 1830-1840. Slightly stylized country painting on an asphaltum ground.
Fig.86

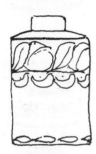

TEA CANISTER. Round. Pennsylvania. 1825-1835. 4 1/4" x 5 1/2". Country painting on a white band with a yellow brush-stroke border. On asphaltum.
Fig.87

TEA CANISTER. Oval. Connecticut. 1834. 4 1/4" high, 3 3/8" wide, and 2 5/8" deep. Country painting on asphaltum. A scratched signature and date on the bottom: "Elizabeth Ely. 1934."
Fig.88

TEA CANISTER. Cylindrical. New England. 1830's. 4 1/4" x 8 1/2". Country painting on asphaltum. Red, green, and yellow.
Fig.89

TEA CANISTER. Sometimes called
STEEPLE-TOP CANISTER. Massachusetts.
1851. 5" x 8 3/4". The design is
stenciled on an asphaltum background.
"Bliss' Patent 1851" is stamped in
tin.   Fig.90

TEA CANISTER. England. 1870's.
2 1/2" x 2 1/2" x 5". One of many
exported items. Crystalized blue
background with a printed pattern.
                                  Fig.91

TEA CANISTER. England. Circa 1865.
12" x 9" x 28". Made for Japanese
tea. A painted scene, gold-printed
scroll, and bronze striping on a
black background   Fig.92

TEA CANISTER. England. Circa 1870-
1880. 12" x 8" x 27". Tin-printed
flower painting and a gold design on
a black ground.   Fig.93

CHAMBER WARE

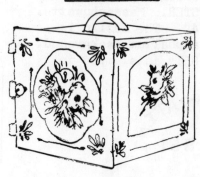

POT BOX. England. Circa 1860. 9" x 6 1/2" square.
Painted design with a stenciled border on the four sides
of this white box.   Fig.94

SLOP PAIL. Boston. Circa 1870.
12 1/2". From the Dover Stamping Co.
"Boston" pattern in red, green, and
blue flowers in the panel.   Fig.95

TUB or FOOT BATH. England. 1860's.
22" x 10". Moss roses on a white
background. The tub is lined with
blue paint.   Fig.96

TUB or FOOT BATH. Midlands, England.
1860's. 38" x 9". Painted-metal,
leaf design on the rim.   Fig.97

TUB or FOOT BATH. Boston.   1870.   26" x 9" x 10". From
the Dover Stamping Company.   "Boston" pattern, red, green,
blue, and gold.   Fig.98

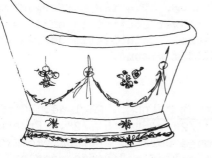

TUB or SITZBATH. England. Circa 1840. 24"
long, 32" at highest point. The design is
late, non-descriptive flower painting. Enamel apron.   Fig.99

WATER CARRIER. Midland, England.
1850-1860. 9" at base, 12 1/4"
tall, 8 3/4" at top. Moss rose
design painted on white background.   Fig.100

WATER CARRIER. Boston. 1870. 9" diameter at base, 12 1/4" tall. "Boston"
pattern in red, gold, green, and blue.
                                       Fig.101

CHEESE CRADLES

CHEESE CRADLE. Pontypool, Wales.
Circa 1795. 6" deep, 12" tall, 3" x
9" base. The top half revolves into
the lower section to enclose the
cheese. Chinoiserie design on asphaltum ground.   Fig.102

CHEESE CRADLE. England. Circa 1845.
13 1/2" x 6" x 5 1/2". Freehand
bronze work on a black background.
Not called a "cheese coaster."
                                       Fig.103

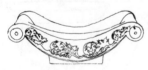

CHEESE CRADLE. England. Circa 1850.
13 1/2" x 6" x 5 1/2". The design is
a negative stencil on a black background. Two section cradle. Fig.104

CHEESE CRADLE. England. Late 1800's.
14" long. Called "an improved piece"
in the trade. Decorative painting.
                                       Fig.105

CHESTS FOR TEA

TEA CHEST. England. Circa 1765.
Bombé shape with chinoiserie design
on a tortoise-shell background.
Fig.106

TEA CHEST. England. 1790. Pierced
apron on a bombé-shaped chest. 10"
long. Lace-edge painting with fine
gold leaf borders. Brass handle.
Fig.107

COAL VASES

COAL VASE. Miscalled a "coal hod."
Wolverhampton, England. Circa 1844.
21" x 24" x 15". Stamped-out piece.
So-called "Chippendale" painting on
a black background. Typical Wolverhampton product.   Fig.108

COAL VASE. Wolverhampton, England.
Circa 1860. 21" x 20" x 14". Metal
leaf; crude workmanship.   Fig.109

COAL VASE. Wolverhampton, England. 1862. Made by the
Jones Brothers. Octagonal, black, with a reverse painting on glass panel on top.   Fig.110

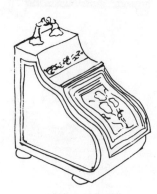

COAL VASE. Southern England. Edwardian period. 21" x 21". Bombé
front with reverse painting on glass
panel and some gold leaf work. Lifts
up in front.   Fig.111

COAL VASE or COAL SCUTTLE. England.
Circa 1850. Victorian style, with a
convex painted-glass inset and a
drawer at the bottom.   Fig.112

COAL VASE or COAL SCUTTLE. Wolverhampton, England. 1862.
There is a transfer design on the sides and a metal leaf
design on the concave glass front. The export pieces had
tin panels rather than glass because they were safer for
shipping.   Fig.113

Top view

PURDONIUM (COAL VASE). France. Mid-1800's. 24" high,
12" across top. Red background. Realistic painting by
an artist (pastoral scene), with gold bronze brush-stroke
border. Top lifts up on hinges. Sometimes found with
aperture in back for shovel.   Fig.114

COMPOTE. England. 1790. 11 1/4" x
7" x 4". Gold leaf and freehand
bronze design, using four shades of
bronze. Brass handles and black
background.   Fig.115

CUPS

MEASURING CUP. One-half pint. Connecticut. Early 1800's. Country
painting: yellow, red, and green on
asphaltum. 4 1/2" high.   Fig.116

MEASURING CUP. Pint measure. Connecticut. Circa 1840. 3" wide x 5"
high. Typical Connecticut country
painting, symmetrical design on asphaltum.   Fig.117

MOLASSES CUP. Sometimes called a
"syrup jug." New England and Pennsylvania. Circa 1830. 4" tall, 3"
across, with a lid. Country painting
on top and sides.   Fig.118

SCHOOL CUP. New England. Late
1800's. 3" tall. Stenciled scroll
with the name painted on it. Red
background.   Fig.119

TOY CUP. Connecticut. Circa 1800.
2 1/4" tall, 2 1/2" wide. Red brush
strokes on asphaltum.   Fig.120

EGG CODDLERS

<u>EGG CODDLER</u>. England. Circa 1840.
5 1/2" x 3 3/4" x 3 1/2". Gold leaf
on a black background.   Fig.121

Detail: inside of Fig.121.   Fig.121A

<u>EGG CODDLER</u>. Pennsylvania. Circa
1840. 4 1/4" tall. Country painting on a red background.   Fig.122

<u>HAT PLATE</u>. For a fireman's helmet.
Circa 1830. Black background with
gold and freehand bronze design. The
hat was sometimes earlier than the
tin plate.   Fig.123

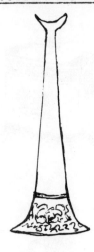

HORNS OR SPEAKING TRUMPETS

HORN or SPEAKING TRUMPET. England.
1853-1896. Used along the canals.
The mouthpiece is typically English.
Design in metal leaf.   Fig.124

HORN. Connecticut. 1850's. Made
of imported tin and painted in America. Used by tin peddlers and fire-
men. Yellow and red brush strokes
on black asphaltum.   Fig.125

INKWELL. France. Circa 1810.
Tray: 6 1/2" x 4 1/2" x 1". Bottle:
2 1/4". The octagonal tray and inkwell are in one piece and on ball
feet. The gallery of the tray is
pierced.   Fig.126

This is one of the few examples we have found of what we
believe is French lace-edge type painting. There are
subtle differences between the English and French styles.
The French colors are slightly flatter and chalkier, and
the designs are airier. The strokes in the French designs do not flow together as do the English strokes.
The background color of this inkwell is yellow -- a rather typical French background color, not found as background in English lace-edge painting.

JARDINIÈRE. France. Circa 1841.
12" x 6 1/2". Claw feet. Delicate-
ly painted scene in brown on a yellow
background.   Fig.127

LAMP FILLER. Pennsylvania. 19th
century. 5 1/2" tall, 3 3/4" at base,
spout is 6" long. Country painting.
Blue flowers with green and yellow
brush strokes. It is unusual to
find one decorated.   Fig.128

TRAVEL LAMP. New England. 1865.
3 1/2" x 3 1/2" x 6 1/4" high. Stenciled on asphaltum, patented, and made
in different sizes.   Fig.129

LAVABO. England. Circa 1845. Tank
is 23 3/8" x 11 3/4" x 6 1/2". Water
catch is 14 1/4" x 11" x 5". The
top is pierced and has a wooden finial. Black background. Beautiful
flower painting with bird and gold
leaf. Owner: HSEAD.   Fig.130

MACHINES

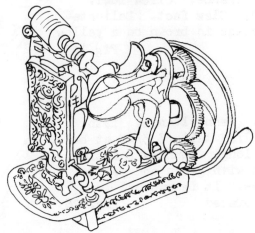

SEWING MACHINE. American, New York. Circa 1858. 8"
high, 7 1/2" long, 3 1/4" wide. Handle 2" beyond length.
Flower design painted on face plate and platform. Metal
leaf scrolls painted on the borders. Many of these models had decals. This one was hand painted, with much
yellow striping.   Fig.131

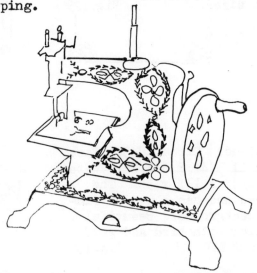

SEWING MACHINE. Germany. Circa 1860. 8" long x 7 1/2"
high x 4 1/4" wide. Black background with metal leaf
and pink painted design.   Fig.132

TYPEWRITER. American. Crandall Model 3. Before 1893.
U. S. Patent 1881 #251338. Hand decorated with pearl
shell and gilt scrolls. Blue, red, and green washes
over design. Black background.   Fig.133

MANTEL ORNAMENT. In the manner of
George Morland. Pontypool, Wales.
Circa 1785. The figure has been
painted on a black japanned cut-out
sheet of metal and mounted on a narrow rectangular japanned box which
has gold-line marbleizing and is
heavily weighted.   Fig.134

MATCH HOLDER. American. Circa 1835.
7 3/4" tall, 4" wide, 1 3/8" deep.
The top is fluted. Yellow brush
strokes on asphaltum background.
                         Fig.135

MATCH SAFE. England. 1860's.
4 1/2" x 2 3/4" x 4". Stenciled on
black asphaltum.   Fig.136

MONTEITH. Pontypool, Wales. Circa
1785. 11" x 8 1/4" x 4 3/4".
Unusual bowl, notched rim, used for
chilling wine glasses. Also called
a "verrière." Brass handles. Lace-
edge painting on a tortoise-shell
background.   Fig.137

MONTEITH. Usk, Wales. Circa 1820.
11" x 8 1/4" x 4 3/4". Gilt design,
black background, also found with a
red background.   Fig.138

MONEY BALANCES & WEIGHT CASE. Pontypool, Wales. Circa 1795. 6 1/2"
long, 3" wide, and 1" deep. Lace-
edge painting on a black background.
                                Fig.139

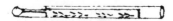 

NEEDLE CASES. Connecticut. Circa 1849. 8 3/4" x 7/16"
diameter, and 12" x 1" diameter. Red and yellow brush-
stroke design on black asphaltum.   Fig.140

PAIL or BLICKY. Pennsylvania.
1850's. 2 1/4" x 1 1/4". A toy,
either stenciled on a blue background
or country-painted on a black background. This one has a white and
green flower with yellow strokes on
top. (The Dutch word blikje means
"tin.")   Fig.141

CREAM PITCHER. American. 1823. 5"
tall, 3 1/2" base. Sometimes found
with a lid. May also be called a
"creamer" or "cream jug." Country
painting on a black background.
Fig.142

CREAM PITCHER. Holland. Hallmarked
before 1750. Pewter and hexagonal in
shape. 6 1/4" tall, 3 3/4" wide, ex-
cluding the handle. Extremely rare.
Evidently decorated by a Pontypool
painter. Lace-edge painting, gold
leaf borders. Background has a tortoise-shell feeling -- a red glow
gleaming through the Brunswick black
background.   Fig.143

POTS

CHOCOLATE POT or SIDE POURER. Connecticut. 19th century. 4 3/4".
4" base. Red, yellow, and green
country painting. The fact that
small side pourers were called chocolate pots came from the China porcelain trade.   Fig.144

COFFEE POT. Pontypool, Wales. Circa
1760. 11". Chinese design in gold
leaf on a tortoise-shell background.
Flame finial.   Fig.145

COFFEE POT. Pontypool, Wales. Circa
1760. 11". Pear-shaped. The strip-
metal handle is covered with basketry.
Lace-edge design on a tortoise-shell
background.   Fig.146

COFFEE POT. England. Circa 1800. 9". Wooden handle, sometimes covered with raffia. Scenic painting in the oval with gold leaf detail. Fig.147

COFFEE POT. American. 1820. 10 1/2" high. Has construction lines and a cone top. Country-painted design. Sometimes referred to as a "lighthouse" coffee pot. Not an authentic term.
Fig.148

COFFEE POT. Connecticut. 1800. 10 3/4". Typical symmetrical design of red, yellow, and green on asphaltum. Good country painting. Fig.149

COFFEE POT. Connecticut. Possibly a Filley piece. Circa 1810. 10 3/4" high. Nice country painting on a dark asphaltum background. Fig.150

COFFEE POT. Crooked spout. From Pennsylvania. 1815. Attributed to Oliver Brunson, a tinsmith who worked for the Filleys. Decorated in the Filley shop. Typical Pennsylvania country painting on asphaltum. 10 3/4" high.
Fig.151

COFFEE POT. Crooked spout. Pennsylvania. Circa 1815. 10 3/4" high.
Also known as a "goose-neck" or
"crooked neck" coffee pot. A product of the Filley shop. Painted
with a pattern requested from the
Connecticut Filley shop for the Pennsylvania trade.   Fig.152

COFFEE POT. Drip variety. Possibly New York. Mid-19th century.
18 1/2" tall, 6 1/4" base. Country
painting in mostly blue and red on
asphaltum.   Fig.153

COFFEE POT. Drip variety. New England. Mid-19th century. 15". Country painting.   Fig.154

COFFEE POT. Maine. Circa 1830.
10 3/4". Typical Maine piece with
flaring spout and wet-on-wet country
painting. The two cherries are
thought to be a Z. Stevens motif.
                               Fig.155

COFFEE POT. Cone top. Pennsylvania.
1820-1830. 12 3/4" high. Pennsylvania tulip design and running borders.
Shape similar to punched coffee pots
that have a design of raised dots,
done before the piece is made.
                               Fig.156

COFFEE POT. Side pourer. Connecticut. 19th century. 10" high, 8" at
base. Red, green, and yellow country
painting on asphaltum.   Fig.157

RACKS

LETTER RACK. Midlands, England.
1860's. 14" x 4 1/2". Gold bronze
scrolls on a black background.
                              Fig.158

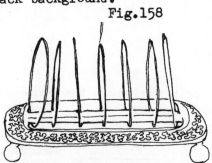

TOAST RACK. Usk, Wales. Circa 1815. 9 1/2" x 3 1/4" x
5". Typical stormont design in gold leaf. Miscalled a
"letter" rack.   Fig.159

SPICE RACK. England. 1852. Imported and sold by Goodridge, Ives &
Rutty Co., Meriden, Connecticut. The
rounded tops are stenciled on asphaltum. 7" x 4 1/2". 4" high.
                              Fig.160

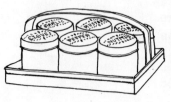

SPICE BOX. American. 1850's. The
flat tops are stenciled with the spice
names and brush strokes on asphaltum.
These were manufactured here and in
England. 7" x 4 1/2". 3 1/2" high.
                              Fig.161

POSTAL SCALES. Chicago. Since 1904. 4 1/2" x 4 3/4". Stenciled in silver on a black background. Design on front plate in center, above.   Fig.162

SHAKERS

FLOUR SHAKER. Connecticut. 1820's. 2 3/4" x 3 1/2". From the Filley shop. Red and yellow country-painting brush strokes.   Fig.163

SAND SHAKER (Ink blotter). American. 1830's. 2 3/4" x 2 7/8". Used to dry ink. Red and yellow brush stroke design.   Fig.164

SNUFFERS or CANDLESHEARS. Pontypool, Wales. 1800-1810. Stormont design on asphaltum background.   Fig.165

SPITTOONS: see BOXES, page 39

TEA KETTLES and TEA POTS

The tea kettle has a swinging handle on top; the teapot has a stationary handle on the side.

TEA KETTLE. Dome top. England.
1800's. 10". Gold leaf border and
a simple painting. Black background.
                                    Fig.166

TEA KETTLE. Pear-shaped. England.
Circa 1800. 11". Fine gold color
background. The accompanying octagonal tray is decorated in gold leaf.
Similar kettles were made in France.
                                    Fig.167

TEAPOT. Maine. Circa 1820. An unusual raised topknot. Heart-shaped
leaves painted in Maine style country painting on a black ground.
                                    Fig.168

TEAPOT. Called "the common pot."
Circa 1820. 5 1/4" high. A popular style, country-painted on black
asphaltum. Also found on colored
grounds.   Fig.169

TEAPOT. Possibly New Hampshire.
Circa 1850. 4 3/4" high. Stenciling
similar to some found in Concord, New
Hampshire. Attributed to George Scrip-
ture. Asphaltum background. Is
sometimes called an "old Maid's" teapot.   Fig.170

TRAYS

Coffin lid trays, or coffin trays, or cut corner trays
are listed under OCTAGONAL TRAYS. The so-called Chippendale trays are listed below as GOTHIC TRAYS. See the
Vocabulary for all definitions.

The GOTHIC TRAY, frequently called a Chippendale tray,
sometimes called a pie-crust tray, originated about
1760. The earliest ones had a flat rim, known as a
sandwich edge, usually with very fine gold-leaf scrolls
coming down onto the floor, or a geometric center design. Occasionally the borders also contain small flowers. In 1800 we find GOTHIC trays with fine gold-leaf
and flower decoration on the floor and flange. From
1840-1850 the designs became larger and the colors more
brilliant. Birds and fountains adorned the trays as
well as bouquets of flowers. Few were made after 1860.

The KING GOTHIC TRAY has a shallow curved, Gothic rim.
Many King Gothic trays had a narrow border of calligraphy.

The cyma curve in the rim of the QUEEN GOTHIC TRAY was
more deeply indented.

Queen Gothic curve.

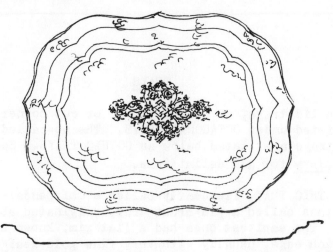

KING GOTHIC TRAY. Sandwich edge. Pontypool, Wales.
1760-1775. 25 1/2" x 20 1/2". The central geometric
design is done in copper and gold leaf, surrounded by a
freehand dull-red design accented with vermillion and
yellow on a brown-black background. Exquisitely striped
in white. See also Fig.256.   Fig.171

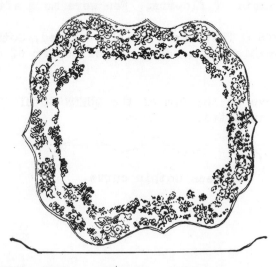

QUEEN GOTHIC TRAY. Midlands, England. Circa 1790-1800.
25 1/2" x 20 1/2". The gold leaf design runs from the
flange onto the floor of the tray, on a black background.
                                                Fig.172

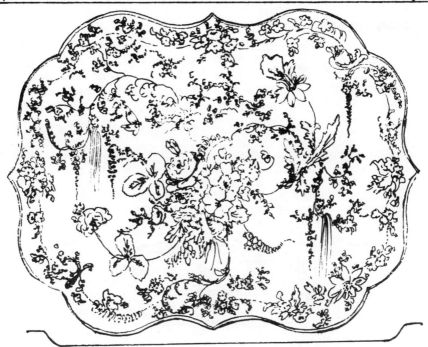

QUEEN GOTHIC TRAY. Sandwich edge. Birmingham, England. Circa 1840. 31" x 24". Black japanned tray with
a dusted bronze background and bronzed clouds. The
painting consists of gold tracery, arabesques, and flowers. Today called "Chippendale" painting.   Fig.173

KING GOTHIC TRAY. Sandwich edge. Circa 1855. 17" x
13 3/4". Transferred gold-leaf scrolls and fine so-called "Chippendale" painting on a black background. Possi-
nly German.   Fig.174

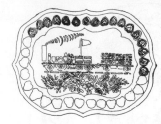

GOTHIC TRAY. Thin edge. Bilston
and Birmingham, England. 1860-1880.
9 1/4" x 12 1/2". Stenciled design
on a black tray. A stamped-on cork
pattern on border.   Fig.175

GOTHIC CARD TRAY. Wolverhampton, England. Circa 1845.
10" in diameter, with brass handle. "Chippendale"
painting of a passion flower, dahlia, and apple blossoms
on a black background. Gold leaf tracery on the flange
and onto the floor.   Fig.176

KIDNEY TRAY. Also called "lap" tray
and "parlor maid's" tray. After
1810. 30 1/2" x 22 1/4". "Chippendale" flower painting with garlands
of fine gold leaf on a black background.   Fig.177

<u>KIDNEY TRAY</u>. England. After 1810. 12" x 9 1/4".
"Chippendale" flower painting and pearl shell on a black
background.   Fig.178

<u>KNIFE TRAY</u>. England. Prior to 1860. 14 3/4" x 4 3/4"
x 2". Sometimes called a "spoon" tray. Miscalled a
"bread" tray. A negative stencil on a black background.
Also found in America with country painting.   Fig.179

<u>ENGLISH OCTAGONAL TRAYS</u>

1765-1820. The earliest had double borders and designs
in gold leaf. The later ones had medallions painted in
natural colors in the tray center, and gold leaf borders.

OCTAGONAL TRAY. Wolverhampton, England. Circa 1810.
32" x 21 1/2" x 2 1/4". Painting of Simon and the In-
fant Christ in the Temple in oval, surrounded by a mar-
gin of gold leaf. Gold-leaf work also on the flange.
Black background. Similar to Joseph Barney's work.
                                                       Fig.180

OCTAGONAL TRAY. Wolverhampton, England. Circa 1780.
28" x 20". Borders in gold leaf; the outer one with
the Greek key and urn pattern, the inner one shells and
sea units. Black background.   Fig.181

OCTAGONAL TRAY. With thin or raw
edge. Midlands, England. Circa
1855. 12 3/8" x 9 1/4" x 1". The
flange has a gold leaf and freehand
bronze design on a black background.
                                Fig.182

OCTAGONAL TRAY. New York. Circa
1830. 12 1/4" x 8 1/2" x 1 1/2".
Country-painted design: red, yellow
and green on a black background. The
naked flange is deeper than on the
usual one-sheet waiter,*otherwise
this could be called a "coffin" tray.
The design is not typical of this particular tray.   Fig.183

OCTAGONAL TRAY. Meriden, Connecticut.
1850. 16 1/2" x 10 3/8" x 1". The
so-called "Berlin" stencil is similar
to those found on tin trunks. Black
asphaltum background.   Fig.184

OCTAGONAL TRAY. New York and Pennsylvania. Circa 1840. 17 1/2" x
13 1/2" x 1 1/4". Country painting on a white band, on a medium
asphaltum background. Note the
narrow hand holes.   Fig.185

* THE OCTAGONAL TRAY or ONE-SHEET WAITER

Sometimes called a "coffin" or "coffin lid" or "cut
corner" tray. Usually has a flange not over 1". The
3/4" flange is the most typical. They are for the most
part 19th century trays, country-painted.

OCTAGONAL TRAY. One-sheet waiter.
Found in New Hampshire. Circa 1850.
12 1/2" x 8 3/4" x 1". This one-
piece stencil is done in two tones
of bronze. The tray has two yellow
stripes. Black background. Fig.186

OCTAGONAL TRAY. One-sheet waiter.
Pennsylvania. Circa 1816. 12 1/2"
x 7 1/2" x 3/4" high. Country painting on a white band. Crystalized
floor and flange.   Fig.187

OCTAGONAL TRAY. Half-sheet waiter.
Connecticut. 1830. 8 3/4" x 5 3/4"
x 5/8". Brush-stroke country painting
on white band. Background of tray is
crystalized. A small "coffin lid" or
cut corner tray.   Fig.188

OCTAGONAL TRAY. Two-sheet waiter. Berlin, Connecticut.
Circa 1815. 17 1/2" x 12" x 1 5/8". Typical Berlin-
type country painting of red, yellow, and green on a dar
asphaltum background.   Fig.189

OVAL TRAYS

OVAL TRAY. England. Early 1800's.
10 1/2" x 7 1/2" x 3/4". Often made
in pairs. Red background with a
gold-leaf border.   Fig.190

OVAL COUNTER TRAY. Pontypool, Wales.
Circa 1780. 3 1/4" x 4 3/8" x 1".
Lace-edge painting on a black back-
ground. Pierced edge.   Fig.191

OVAL TRAY, GALLERY. With hand holes. England. Circa
1790. 24 1/2" x 20" x 2". Gold leaf borders on a black
background.   Fig.192

OVAL TRAY. Pierced gallery. Pontypool, Wales. Circa
1790. 31". Lace-edge painting with a gold-leaf border
close to flange. Tortoise-shell background.   Fig.193

OVAL TRAY. Greenwich, New York. 30". 1860-1878. Probably decorated by Mary Thompson of the American Tray
Works. Two repeated designs of painted gold and green
leaves on a black background. Gold striping. A stamped
tray. Similar trays were imported from England where
they were called "oval Windsor" trays by the japanners.
                                                Fig.194

OVAL TRAY. Greenwich, New York. 1860-1878. 28". Made
at the American Tray Works in that town. Stamped-out
tray. Gold leaf and painted flowers and leaves on a
black background.   Fig.195

OVAL TRAY. Pierced-edge. Pontypool, Wales. Circa
1770. 20" x 15 1/2" x 3/4". Typical lace-edge painting on a tortoise-shell background.   Fig.196

OVAL TRAY. Unpierced edge with brass handles. Pontypool, Wales. Circa 1780. 27" x 18 1/2". Lace-edge
painting on a tortoise-shell background. Gold leaf border on flange.   Fig.197

OVAL TRAY. Unpierced thin edge.
England. Circa 1820. 10 1/4" x
7 3/4". Lace-edge painting on a
black background.   Fig.198

OVAL TRAY. Thin edge. England.
Circa 1860. 11 3/4" x 9 1/4" x 1/2".
The central design is stenciled in
gold. Stamped-on cork border. Black
background.   Fig.199

OVAL TRAY. Thin edge. Wolverhampton, England. 1850's.
12" x 9 1/2". Two cork stamped-on borders separated by
a bronze meandering line.   Fig.200

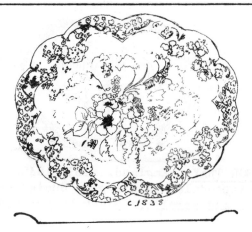

c 1838

OVAL SCALLOPED TRAY. Also called "Victoria" tray. England. Circa 1838. Made exclusively by Ryton & Walton,
Wolverhampton. 20" x 15 1/4" wide. Probably painted by
George Wallis. Gold leaf and flowers on border of black
tray. So-called "Chippendale" painting on a bronze
background covers the center.   Fig.201

OVAL VICTORIAN TRAY. England.
1820-1850. 15" x 12 3/4". Freehand bronzing and transparent
painting on a bronze powder background.   Fig.202

OVAL VICTORIAN TRAY. England.
Circa 1830. 24 1/2" x 20 1/2".
Fine so-called "Chippendale" painting and gold-leaf border. Black
background.   Fig.203

<u>OVAL WINDSOR TRAY</u>. England. 1832-1845. 30" x 19". So-
called "Chippendale" painting on dusted bronze. Gold-
leaf border and scrolls. Black background.   Fig.204

 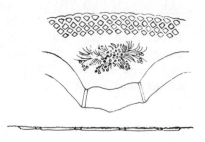

<u>OVAL WINE TRAY</u>. Pontypool, Wales. Circa 1795. Pierced
rim. Brass handles. Lace-edge fruit and flowers on
tortoise-shell background.   Fig.205

<u>QUEEN ANNE TRAY</u>. Circa 1885. Possibly Bilston.
17 1/2" x 14 3/4". Metal leaf scroll border. Design: metal-leaf flowers with transparent alizarin and
green washes.   Fig.206

RECTANGULAR TRAYS   RIM⌐ OR EDGE⌐

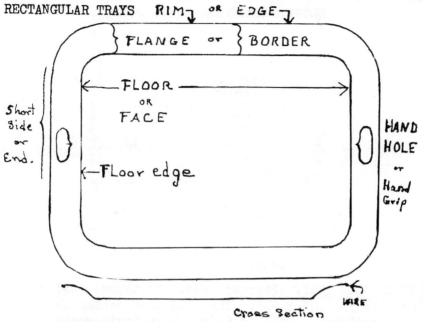

RECTANGULAR TRAY. Curved corner. Fig.207

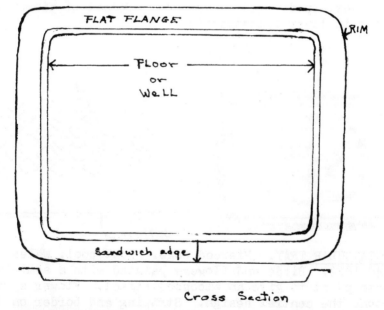

RECTANGULAR TRAY. Sandwich edge. Fig.207A

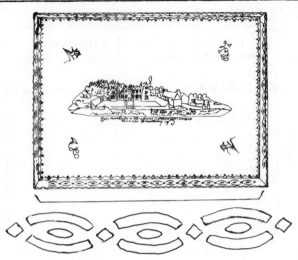

Detail of piercing

RECTANGULAR TRAY. Pierced edge. Pontypool, Wales.
Circa 1755. 28" x 21". The gold leaf design is inscribed "The Old Hall at Kelmersh in Northamphshire."
One of the earliest types of piercing. The corners
are overlapped. Red background. Detail of piercing
shown in lower illustration.   Fig.208

RECTANGULAR TRAY. Pierced edge. Pontypool, Wales.
1740-1822. Birds and flowers painted with a semi-im-
pasto paint to give an embossed effect. Flower sprays
around the central design. Striping and border on the
floor are gold leaf. Detail of the pierced edge at the
right.   Fig.209

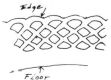

RECTANGULAR TRAY. Pierced edge with rounded corners.
Pontypool, England. Circa 1790. 22 1/2" x 16 1/4". A
rare shape, decorated with a fine gold-leaf border.
Lace-edge painting: peach, flowers, typical small sprays.
                                                    Fig.210

RECTANGULAR TRAY. Unpierced edge. Pontypool, Wales.
Circa 1820. 12" x 7 1/2" Lace-edge painting design
with a stenciled border. Rare.   Fig.211

RECTANGULAR TRAY. Sandwich edge. Midlands, England.
1830-1840. 20 1/2" x 15 3/4". Very fine gold-leaf
scroll border on a black background.   Fig.212

RECTANGULAR TRAY, with rounded corners. Wolverhampton,
England. Circa 1818. 30" x 22 1/2", with a 2 1/2"
flange. The design, which covers the entire tray, is
freehand bronze and painted umber details on a Brunswick black background. Typical George Morland subject.
                                                   Fig.213

RECTANGULAR TRAY, with rounded corners. Wolverhampton,
England. Circa 1800. 32" x 22 1/2". Frequently called
a "bride's tray" because of the delicacy of the pattern,
and many were found on white backgrounds. Design: freehand bronze and gold leaf, running from flange onto the
floor. Backgrounds were in various colors. Similar
style designs found on Pontypool pieces leads us to believe that the "bride's tray" may also have been made in
Pontypool. See also Fig.255.   Fig.214

RECTANGULAR TRAY. Wolverhampton,
England. Circa 1845. 26" x 18 1/2",
with a 2 1/2" flange. Double borders, gold-leafed and painted. The
floor design is in freehand bronze
with fruit in the corners, joined by
flowers and leaves. The flange border has bronzed units and white fan-
like patterns. On a red background.
There is stormont on the flange between the fan motifs and the large
leaves. This type of tray may have
a cream, white, or black background
as well as the red. Frequently called by the generic term "Pontypool,"
this type of tray became a highly
popular Wolverhampton item. Fig.215

RECTANGULAR TRAY. Wolverhampton, England. Mid-1800's.
30" x 22", with 2 1/2" flange. Sizes range from 14 1/4"
x 11" to 31" x 23 1/2". All types of design except lace-
edge painting were found on this style tray. Black background.   Fig.216

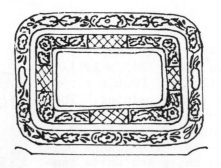

RECTANGULAR TRAY. Wolverhampton, England. Circa 1860.
26" x 20" with a 2 1/2" flange. Metal leaf and free
hand bronze on a red background. On this later tray
the double border design does not have the delicate
freehand bronze stump work as shown in Figs. 215 and
216. Hand holes on large rectangular trays are rarely
opposite each other as in this tray because of the prob-
lem of balancing.   Fig.217

RECTANGULAR TRAY. With rounded corners and hand holes.
Midlands, England. Circa 1850. 22 1/4" x 16". The
flange has 5/8" bronze band. This may be one of their
export items, many of which are varnished only over
the good clean stenciling. Lavender, blue and red
washes over silver stencil design.   Fig.218

RECTANGULAR TRAY. With rounded corners. Midlands, England. Circa 1850 to 1914. 26" x 19 1/2". The scenic
design, "Lady in a Swing," is stenciled, with colored
washes. In the style of paintings by Watteau and Pater.
Black background.   Fig.219

RECTANGULAR TRAY. With rounded corners. Wolverhampton, England. Circa 1860. 29 3/4" x 23 3/4". Hand holes. Background grained to simulate wood; the design is in metal leaf and white paint.   Fig.220

RECTANGULAR TRAY. Thin edge. England. From 1850. 11 3/4" x 8 3/4". A one-piece stencil on the floor, with transparent washes. The border design is stamped on with a cork. See the entry for "Cork Printing" in the chapter on "Inventors and Inventions."   Fig.221

RECTANGULAR TRAY. Thin edge. New England. 1845. 5" x 4" x 1/4". Yellow brush strokes, blue water, and white swan. Black background. A child's toy tray.   Fig.222

ROUND TRAYS

The small pierced-edge tray or "waiter," from 7" to 18"
in diameter, is one of the earliest examples of Pontypool ware. Circa 1740. At the time these round wait-.
ers were more numerous than the rectangular trays.
They usually had a tortoise-shell background and were
painted with flowers and fruit, and had a gold-leaf
border and stripe around the extreme edge of the floor.
Derby porcelain artists, when out of work, painted
Pontypool pierced-edge trays such as these. The Adam
influence is evident in the numerous waiters found
painted with a central urn, intertwined ribbons around
it, often interspersed with sprays of flowers. It was
probably Esther Stevens Brazer who gave these trays the
name "lace-edge" trays because of the lacy effect of
their pierced edges.

ROUND TRAY. Pierced edge. Pontypool, Wales. 1740-
1860. 7 1/4" in diameter. Lace edge with brush strokes
and stripe. The flowers are circled by a green wreath.
Tortoise-shell background.   Fig.223

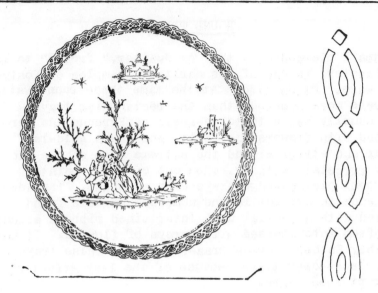

ROUND TRAY. Pierced edge. Pontypool, Wales. Circa
1760-1775. Designs of this type were copied from scenic
paintings of well-known English artists rather than inspired by chinoiseries or oriental motifs. Gold-leaf
design on red background. Early piercing.   Fig.224

ROUND TRAY. Crimped edge. Possibly Usk, Wales. Circa
1850. 9 1/4" in diameter, 3/8" high. Floral design on
a black background. Similar to lace-edge painting.
                                                   Fig.225

ROUND TRAY. Also called a "tea pot
stand." Birmingham, England. Circa
1855. 10 1/4" in diameter. Persian
style decoration on black. Possibly
by James Hinks.   Fig.226

ROUND TRAY. Wolverhampton, England.
1860. 10 1/4" in diameter. The all-
black design is a transfer printed on
a yellow crystalized ground. Fig.227

ROUND TRAY. Midlands, England. Circa
1865. 10" in diameter. Red berries,
gold leaf, and green leaves on black
background. Note the similarity to
American Tea Tray Works' products
and designs.   Fig.228

ROUND CARD TRAY. Sandwich edge.
Birmingham, England. Circa 1860.
10" diameter. Brass handle. Pearl
shell decoration on flange and on
floor; flower painting on black
background .   Fig.229

ROUND SMOKER'S TRAY, SCALLOPED. With
charcoal holder. England. Circa
1780. 10" in diameter. Design in
gold leaf on black background. The
tongs lift the charcoal to the men's
pipes. Before the lucifer match.

Fig.230

ROUND SMOKER'S TRAY. Pierced edge. Pontypool, Wales.
Circa 1780. 10" in diameter. 3 1/2" tall. Lace-edge
painting on black.   Fig.231

RUSSIAN TRAYS

Decorated trays from Zhostovo, a village near Moscow,
appeared first in the middle of the nineteenth century.
The founder of this type tray was the famous Russian
painter, Vishniakov. Today's trays from Zhostvo are
cruder in color and design, but the workmanship is still
exquisite and highly skilled for anything being turned
out in such quantities and so cheaply. Many of these
trays were and still are being imported to the United
States. Those manufactured before the Russian revolution were stamped on the back, "Made in Russia." Since
the revolution they are marked "Made in USSR."

RUSSIAN TRAY. 19th century to present. 15 1/2" x 11 3/4"
x 1". Bright, thin, enamel flower painting augmented by
numerous very fine brush strokes. The backgrounds of
these trays are black, off-red, red, green, or blue.

Fig.232

Made in Russia

RUSSIAN TRAY. 19th century. 15" x 11 3/4". Imprint,
"Made in Russia," on back. Black background, large flow-
ers: pink, red, purple, orange, and blue-green leaves.
Beautiful thin painting. Bronze border.   Fig.233

<u>SERPENTINE TRAY</u>. Midlands, England. 1850's. 20" x
14 1/2". Early stenciling and fine stump work. Wide
bronze stripe on the flange. Black background. Fig.234

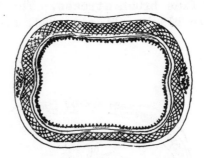

<u>SERPENTINE TRAY</u>. Birmingham, England. Circa 1835. 15"
x 12 1/2". Double border design in metal leaf. The hand
grips are hidden on the underside of the tray. Black
background.   Fig.235

<u>SNUFFERS TRAY</u>. Wolverhampton, Eng-
land. From 1760. 9 1/2" x 3 3/4"
x 1/2". A design frequently called
by the generic term "Pontypool."
Originated in Wolverhampton. Stormont gold-leaf units and painting
over a gold-leaf band. Black background.   Fig.236

SNUFFERS TRAY. Usk, Wales. Circa
1845. 8 1/2" x 3 7/8". A painted
scene, stormont, cross-hatching
over gold leaf, on a red background.
Fig.237

SNUFFERS TRAY. Wolverhampton, England. Circa 1830. 9 1/2" x 4 1/4"
x 1/2". Transparent painting over
the gold leaf background on this
black tray.   Fig.238

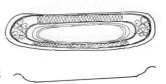

SNUFFERS TRAY. Boat-shaped, American.
1810-1830. 9 3/8" x 3 1/2" x 1/2".
Country painting on black.   Fig.239

SNUFFERS TRAY. Connecticut. 1845.
8 1/4" x 3 1/4" x 1/4". The oval
ends are crimped. Red, yellow, and
green country painting on a black
background.   Fig.240

SNUFFERS TRAY. Gothic shape. Wolverhampton, England. Circa 1800.
10 1/4" x 5". The shell pattern: gold
leaf with painting on a cream background. Design after Robert Hancock.
Fig.241

SNUFFERS TRAY. Keyhole shape. Wolverhampton, England. Circa 1842-
1850. Also called a "stepped edge"
snuffers tray. Signed "Benjamin &
Walton, Wolverhampton, England."
Flat edge, concave flange, stamped-
out piece. Design: flower painting
on a blue background.   Fig.242

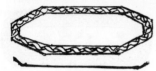

SNUFFERS TRAY. Octagonal. American.
1810-1845. 9 1/4" x 3 3/4" x 1/2".
A country painting brush stroke border on a black background.   Fig.243

SNUFFERS TRAY. Octagonal, thin edge.
Wolverhampton, England. Circa 1850.
9 1/4" x 3 3/4" x 1/2". Freehand
bronze corners, leaf pattern at ends.
White striping. Red ground. Fig.244

TRUNKS

These trunks were sometimes called spice, trinket, deed,
document, or money boxes, depending on their size.

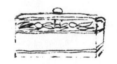

TIN TRUNK. Connecticut. Circa 1823.
6 1/2" x 3" x 3 1/2". Small dome
top. White band with red and green
brush strokes and an asphaltum background.   Fig.245

TIN TRUNK. Dome top. New York. Circa 1824. 9" x 6 1/4". Butler piece.
Country painting. White bands on
top. Asphaltum ground.   Fig.246

TIN TRUNK. Dome top. New York.
Circa 1824. 8 3/4" x 4 3/4".
Possibly painted by Mercy North.
Red bands with brush strokes in
green on top. Other borders are
yellow brush strokes. Asphaltum
background with a feather graining
of black paint on top. (Zigzag
pattern)   Fig.247

TIN TRUNK. Flat top. Stevens Plains,
Maine. Circa 1810. 9" x 5" x 6". Wet-
on-wet painting, which is unlike the
country painting from other states.
This type box came in all sizes.
Green brush stroke border on a yellow
ground.   Fig.248

TIN TRUNK. Maine. 1800-1842.
9 3/4" x 6" x 7 1/4". Platform top,
brass handle, country painting with
black rick-rack on a red background.
                                     Fig.249

TIN TRUNK. Maine. 1815-1820.
Signed M.A.B. Attributed to Oliver Buckley, a gift to his daughter Mary Ann.   Fig.249A

TIN TRUNK. Connecticut. 1830-1850.
8 1/2" x 5" x 5 1/4". Gothic top
stamped out. Brass handle. One-
piece stencil on a transparent blue
background. Top striped.   Fig.250

TIN TRUNK. Flat top. Possibly from
Meriden, Connecticut. Circa 1850.
8 1/2" x 4 1/2" x 4 3/4". One-piece
stencil, color washes and stripes.
Considered a typical stencil of the
Berlin shops.   Fig.251

TUMBLER. American. Circa 1800's.
4" tall, 3" at top, 2 1/4" at bottom.
Asphaltum background. Country brush
strokes, red and yellow. The same
template, turned upside down, made
the molasses cup.   Fig.252

TUREENS

TUREEN. Pontypool, Wales. Circa
1770. 10 1/2" long, 8" tall. Lovely pierced rim, acorn finial on lid,
and brass handles. Lace-edge painting on a tortoise-shell background.
                                 Fig.253

TUREEN. Pontypool, Wales. Circa
1775. 9" x 4 1/2" x 7" high. The
handles and finial are brass; the
design: lace-edge painting on tortoise-shell background.   Fig.254

URNS

CHESTNUT URN. Pontypool, or Usk, Wales.   Circa 1773.
12 1/2" high. Pewter. Lion-head handles. Black background. The delicate "bride's tray" type design in
gold leaf leads us to believe that the so-called "bride's
tray" may have been made in Wales before it became popular in the Midlands. See also Fig.214.   Fig.255

CHESTNUT URN. Pontypool, Wales.
1760-1775. 12 1/2" high. Acorn
finial and lion-head handles. A
copper and gold-leaf geometric design over dull red. Informal units,
accented with vermilion and yellow.
found "hit or miss" throughout the
brown-black background. Striped in
white. See the King's Gothic tray
shown in Fig.171.   Fig.256

CHESTNUT URN. Pontypool, Wales. 1790.
12 1/2". Lion-head handles and an
acorn finial. The design is in freehand bronze on Brunswick black.
                              Fig.257

CHESTNUT URN. Pontypool, Wales.
1780-1820. 11 3/4". This unusual
shaped urn has fine gold-leaf work on
a black background.   Fig.258

CHESTNUT URN. France. 1780-1810.
12 1/2". Very similar to the English
urns. Umber painting on a white
background. The gold leaf borders
are over very dark brown background.
                              Fig.259

COFFEE URN. Pontypool, Wales. Circa
1800. 16". Interesting piercing for
ventilation. A cavity in the back
for a spirit lamp, and a tap in front.
The wide oak leaf border is done in
gold leaf on a black background. The
decoration is said to be by Thomas
Barker. See also Fig.57.   Fig.260

COFFEE URN. With brazier. England.
1810. 14 1/2" high. There is a
pastoral scene painted on a black
background with a gold leaf border.
In the manner of Thomas Barker.
                                    Fig.261

HOT WATER URN. With handle. England.
Circa 1827. 12 3/4" high. Scenic
paint-and-bronze painting in the manner of Thomas Barker. Gold leaf border of an oak leaf pattern. Black
background. Holland pieces were more
pear-shaped and bulbous and usually
had two handles.   Fig. 262

HOT WATER URN. England. 18th century.
10 3/4" high. Similar to Dutch urns,
this pewter urn has gold-leaf decorations on a black background. Handle
in back.   Fig.263

TEA URN. Pontypool, England. Circa
1770. One side of the perforated
plinth is hinged to allow insertion
of a brazier. Black japanned, with
a superimposed red ground. Fruit,
flowers, and bullfinch in naturalis-
tic colors. Lace-edge painting.
                                   Fig.264

Detail of pierced base.   Fig.264A

WALNUT DISH. Connecticut. 1840.
3". Country painting. Attributed
to the Filley Shop. Asphaltum background.   Fig.265

WARMERS

FOOT WARMER. America. Mid-19th
century. 7" square. Design stenciled on a black background.   Fig.266

PAP WARMER. Connecticut. Circa
1863. 8 1/4" high, 4 1/4" round.
Burner "C" fits inside lower door.
Small pan "B" sits inside "A", which
holds water. They fit into the top
of the warmer. Design stenciled on
an asphaltum background. Sometimes
found on transparent blue and semi-
transparent green.   Fig.267

A   B   C

PAP WARMER or NURSE'S LAMP. England.
1850. Made for export. The design
is stenciled. This has the "A" and
"B" units shown in Fig.267. Note
the handles. Piece did not have a
door.   Fig.268

PLATE WARMER. Pontypool, Wales. Circa 1785. Lace-edge painting on a black background.   Fig.269

PLATE WARMER. England. Circa 1820. 30". Cabriole legs and lion-head handles. Gold-leaf design on a red background.   Fig.270

PLATE WARMER. Midlands, England. 27" high. Dark red piece. Lion-head handles, snake-foot cabriole legs. Design: negative stenciling on a black border. 13" wide, $10\frac{1}{2}$" deep.   Fig.271

WINE COASTER or BOTTLE STAND. Birmingham, England. Circa 1810. 6"
round, 1 1/2" deep. Chinoiserie or
Pillement design. Usually found in
pairs with red, yellow, or black
backgrounds.   Fig.272

WINE COOLER. Possibly French. Circa
1810. Double piercing at top, lion-
head handles. Flower painting on a
white circular ground. Black background.   Fig.273

WINE COOLER. Holland. Circa 1810.
11" tall, 8" wide. The cooler is
black, with a water scene painted on
a white ground. Note the similarity
to the French cooler.   Fig.274

ACCESSORIES
in
PAPIER-MACHE

Prior to 1772 the French word "papier-mâché" was used in English-speaking countries. It was Henry Clay who introduced the word "paperware" following the patenting of his invention for layering paper in 1772. After 1825, Jennens & Bettridge reintroduced the more fashionable word -- "papier-mâché."

Papier-mâché articles were designed chiefly to catch the feminine eye. The intention was to dazzle. It was produced for a variety of purposes, some surprisingly sturdy. Work stands, cabinets, tables, and chairs were introduced in parlors, giving the drawing room an ornate ambiance. It was even attempted to construct houses and train wheels of papier-mâché, plans that were soon abandoned. However, for the elegant accessory, the material remained popular. It was introduced in England in the 18th century and by 1770 was well established in Birmingham where it became a separate and lucrative trade. (See "Henry Clay" under "Manufacturers and Manufactories.")

BED. Birmingham, England. Circa 1830. 8' 11 1/2" tall. The papier-mâché panels are decorated with gold-leaf scrolls and so-called "Chippendale" painting. Bronze and metal leaf was used on the japanned metal posts. This is known as a "half tester bed."   Fig.275

BELLOWS. Birmingham, England. 1835. 17". Made by
Jennens & Bettridge. Mother-of-pearl and gold leaf on
a black background.   Fig.276

SNUFF BOX. European. 1790. 3 1/2"
x 2" x 1 1/2". Polychrome enamel
painted scene in soft, natural colors. Japanned black, ribbed sides.
                              Fig.277

TRINKET BOX or CASKET. Birmingham,
England. 1830-1850. The design is
a painting of Windsor Castle. The
borders are gold leaf over transparent red color on a japanned black
background. The four corners have
imitation buhl. 10" wide x 5" deep,
by 3" high. Possibly painted by
John Thomas.   Fig.278

WORK BOX. Birmingham, England. 1825. By Jennens &
Bettridge. 18 3/4" x 13" x 7 1/2". The design is pearl
shell, tinted. Gilded scroll borders on a japanned
background.   Fig.279

CARD CASE. Birmingham, England.
1846. 2 1/4" x 3 1/2". Clustered
pearl shell buildings, by John Alsager. His partner, George Neville,
did the small amount of painting on
this piece.   Fig.280

RULE CASE. Midlands, England. Circa
1860. 10 1/2"long. Oriental design
in gilt on black.   Fig.281

SPECTACLE CASE. Birmingham, England.
1852-1872. 6 3/4". Done in the
Sheldon Shop. Transfer print on a
black ground.   Fig.282

CHAIR. Wood and papier-mâché. Midlands, England.
Circa 1840. Groups of flowers, scrolls and arabesques,
gilt on black with some pearl shell. Painting of War-
wick Castle on chair back.   Fig.283

CORNER SHELF. Midlands, England.
1860's. 7 1/2" tall, 5" from center
out. Oriental gilt design with pale
enamel slightly raised faces. Black
background.   Fig.284

FINGER PLATE. Also called DOOR PLATE. Birmingham, England. Circa 1825. 10 1/4" x 3".
"Chippendale" painting on a dusted bronze
background. A signed piece. The actual size
and position of the signatures are as shown
below   Fig.285

JENNENS & BETTRIDGE

FRAME. Birmingham, England. Circa 1860. 13" x 12".
Pearl shell on gilt design with color washes over the
pearl. Black background.   Fig.286

INKSTAND. Birmingham, England. 1855.
8" x 5" x 5 1/2". Black background.
Design in gold leaf. Bottles are cut
glass. Center box for wafers. A
concave space for pens in front.
                                   Fig.287

MATCH-HOLDERS

MATCH-HOLDER. Birmingham, England.
1850. 3". Metal leaf design.
Glass-paper is glued to the base.
                                   Fig.288

MATCH-HOLDER. Birmingham, England.
1850-1860. 3 1/4". Metal leaf
oriental-type design on a black
background.   Fig.289

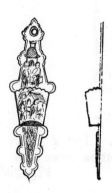

MATCH-HOLDER. Birmingham, England.
1870. 8" x 2 1/2" x 1 3/8". Metal
leaf design on a black background.
The scalloped top of the match holder in the middle has glass paper beneath it. Slightly raised faces.
Illustration shows front and side
views.   Fig.290

MUSIC CANTERBURY. With scrolls and pearl shell on the
drawer and sides. Birmingham, England. Circa 1855.
30" x 10" x 24". So-called "Chippendale" painting and
gold leaf. This carved music holder has pear knobs
and ribbed ball feet.   Fig.291

CARD or LETTER RACK. Birmingham, England. 1846. 15"
tall, 9" wide. Metal leaf scroll border with so-called
"Chippendale" painting in the center. A McCallum and
Hodgson product. Black background.   Fig.292

LETTER RACK. Midlands, England. 1860. 6 1/2" x 2 7/8" x 6". A late oriental-type design, gilt on black. Design flat, not in relief.
Fig.293

PAPER RACK. Birmingham, England. 1845. 6" x 3 1/4" x 5". A Gothic-shaped piece. So-called "Chippendale painting on black.   Fig.294

PAPER RACK, from the Litchfield Manufacturing Co. 1850-1854. 6 1/2" x 3 3/4" x 6 1/2". Pearl shell and gilt decoration on black. Gothic shape.   Fig.295

ROUNDEL. France. 18th century. 7" in diameter. An ornament. Chinoiserie design in gilt on a black ground.   Fig.296

SCREENS

HAND SCREEN. Miscalled a "face fan."
Birmingham, England. 1847. 11" x
7" with 10" handle. Gold-leaf
scrolls, so-called "Chippendale"
painting on a cream background.
This shape was used by McCallum and
Hodgson.   Fig.297

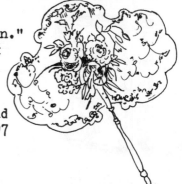

POLE or FIRE SCREEN. Birmingham,
England. 1830-1840. 52" tall.
Tripod decorated with gold scrolls.
The screen has a painting of the sun
setting over Dunstaffnage Castle.
                            Fig.298

POLE or FIRE SCREEN. Birmingham,
England. Circa 1864. Gilt decoration in the Watteau style. These
screens were rectangular, Gothic,
round, and various other shapes.
                    Fig.299

SIDES

BLOTTER SIDE or STATIONERY CASE.
1860. Jennens & Bettridge. 8" x
6". Many colors make up the design,
which is outlined with heavy metal
leaf lines.   Fig.300

BOOK SIDES. Possibly Torrington, Connecticut. 1851-1861. 7 1/2" x 5". Design: metal leaf tracery, pearl shell flowers with color washes.   Fig.301

DAGUERREOTYPE SIDES or CASE. Litchfield Manufacturing Company, Connecticut. 1851. Pearl shell (imported from England) under transparent painted roses. Leaves and stems gilt, with transparent washes. Black background.   Fig.302

PORTFOLIO SIDES. Birmingham, England. 1835. 9" x 10". Pearl shell design on a black background, with flower painting.   Fig.303

TABLES

END TABLE. Birmingham, England. 1850. 19" long, 14" wide and 27" high. A floral design on dusted bronze, with an arabesque border. So-called "Chippendale" painting. Gold leaf sprays on wooden frame. Black background   Fig.304

SEWING TABLE. England. 18th century. Black lacquered piece, with
sewing bag. Chinoiserie design.
Fig.305

TRIPOD, TILT-TOP, or TIP-UP TABLE.
Midlands, England. 1830-1850. 29"
tall. Fine so-called "Chippendale"
painting with a gold-leaf scroll
border.   Fig.306

TRAYS

CARD TRAY. Oxford, England. Circa 1837. 10". Painted
by Spiers & Son. Oxford scene on the floor of the tray.
Gilt border on the front and back flange. Ormolu handle.
Fig.307

COUNTER TRAYS

These 18th and 19th century small trays held counters
for games. They came in sets.

COUNTER TRAY. England. 4 3/4" x
3" x 1". Gold leaf and stenciled
border on a red ground.   Fig.308

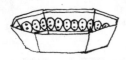

COUNTER TRAY. 4 1/2" x 3 1/4" x 1"
deep. Red background, black stripe
and design over gold leaf. Fig.309

COUNTER TRAY. Stamped "Wonter &
Benson, London." Listed 1802-1805.
4 1/4" x 3 1/4" x 1". Black with
gold leaf design. Concave outside.
                                Fig.310

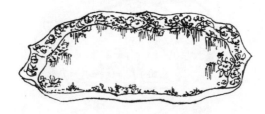

GOTHIC TRAY. England. 1770-1812. 31" x 22 3/4" x 2".
A signed "Henry Clay" piece. Exquisite so-called "Chippendale" painting and gold-leaf work on black background.
                                                Fig.311

GOTHIC TRAY. With narrow sandwich edge. Birmingham,
England. Circa 1840. 17" x 13 1/4". So-called "Chippendale" painting, fine gold-leaf border. Black background.   Fig.312

PARLOR-MAID TRAY. Birmingham, England. Circa 1849.
25" x 16". Made by Jennens & Bettridge. Painted shells
and metal leaf border on a black background.   Fig.313

RECTANGULAR TRAY. Midlands, England.
Circa 1805. 14 1/4" x 11". The
background is japanned black with a
freehand bronze design of foliage
and flowers.   Fig.314

RUSSIAN TRAY. Circa 1880. About 6" in diameter.
Signed with a fine brush, in English vermillion, "Factory N. Lukutin," in Cyrillic lettering, and stamped
three times with the gold double-eagle seal the factory
used. In its earliest years it used one seal, later
two, then three, and finally four seals. In 1900 the
factory closed down but was revived by its craftsmen
and became known as the Artel of Fedoskino. Today it
is one of the best known producers of Russian lacquer.

Russian lacquer work dates back to the 18th century and
has been continuous to the present day. The famous
Lukutin lacquer was destined not only for home use but,
in the first half of the 19th century was exported to
Italy, Germany, and Sweden, finally also to the United
States, where fine examples such as this one keep turning up.

The Russians decorated chests, snuff- and match-boxes,
brooches, candlesticks, inkstands, Easter eggs, covers
for albums, and notebooks, vases, dishes, trays, and
other objects made of wood, papier-mache, or tin. Some
miniatures were worked on a pearl shell base. The picture on the tray shown here is after a painting by K.A.
Trutovsky -- by a copyist therefore -- and the date is
approximately 1880. It is described in I.N. Ukhanova's
book, Russian Lacquer in the Hermitage, and is called
"Rendez-vous."   Fig.315

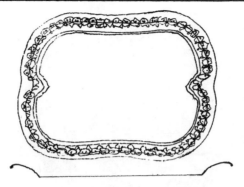

SERPENTINE TRAY. Birmingham, England. Circa 1875.
20" x 14". Transfer metal leaf border on a black
background. The hand grips are hidden on the underside
of the tray.   Fig.316

SNUFFERS TRAY. Birmingham, England.
Circa 1810. 10 1/2" x 4 1/4".
Freehand bronze design outlined in
gold leaf. Red washes. Black
background.   Fig.317

TEA BOARD (TRAY). Birmingham, England. Circa 1800.
32 1/4" x 23 1/4". A brilliant stenciled pattern. The
floor is nailed to the sides of the table, and the two
fine stripes on the back of the 3-inch high flange indi-
cate an early tray.   Fig.318

VICTORIAN TRAY. Birmingham, England. Circa 1840.
29 1/2" x 23". So-called "Chippendale" flower painting
with peacock and fountain on dusted bronze ground.
Arabesque gold leaf border. Black background. Signed
Jennens and Bettridge. The border is typical of that
firm.   Fig. 319

WINDSOR TRAY. Wolverhampton, England. Circa 1846.
22" x 16 1/2". Painted by Edwin Haselar. Flower design of pelargoniums, done naturalistically with leaves
in gold leaf and bronzes.   Fig. 320

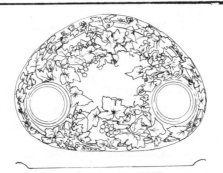

WINE or SUPPER TRAY. Wolverhampton, England. Circa
1830-1840. 32". The unusual fan shape is painted with
grapes and leaves on a black background. Note the two
indented round sections to hold wine glasses.   Fig.321

VASES

VASE. Birmingham, England. Circa
1848. 24" high. So-called "Chippendale" painting. A peacock on one
side, flowers on the other over
dusted bronze. A dark green vase
with fine arabesques.   Fig.322

SPILL VASE. Midlands, England.
1860-1870. 4 3/4" tall, 3" at base
of flange. Late oriental metal leaf
painting on a black background.
                            Fig.323

WALNUT DISH. Birmingham, England.
Circa 1825. 5" x 3" x 1 1/2".
Possibly done by Joseph Booth who
was employed by Jennens & Bettridge.
Exquisite Chinese decoration in
gilt. A little larger than a counter
tray and not found in sets. Fig.324

WINE COASTER or BOTTLE STAND. England, 1820. 5 1/4" x 1 1/2". Freehand bronze and gold leaf on a red
background. These usually come in
pairs.   Fig.325

ACCESSORIES
in
WOOD

BARREL. New York. Circa 1825.
25" x 12". Yellow and brown eagle
with green ribbon. Possibly made
to commemorate the 1825 opening of
the Lake Erie Canal.   Fig.326

BELLOWS

Few examples of bellows are found prior to the 18th century. However, according to writings, there are refer-
ences to bellows that date back to 200 B.C. Anarchar-
sis, a Scythian prince, is said to have been their inventor. A kind of leather bellows is known to have been
used in Egypt a thousand years before that.

Leather from cows, oxen, and goats is used to make bellows.

Most of today's examples were made in the nineteenth
century. The early, old English name was "blow-bag."
Paul Revere imported turned wood, leather, and brass
bellows from England. In 1811, Albany, New York, had
a brush and bellows manufacturing company. Charles
McMurty made bellows and sold them in Connecticut and
Massachusetts. Eckstein & Richardson of Philadelphia
made bellows about 1820. They were labeled "Eckstein
& Richardson Phil Penn." Many bellows were made in
America and England, as well as in other countries.

The various shapes were round, rectangular, heart-,
and pear-shaped. Simple bellows did not have the brass
nozzle nor the braided or woven leather decoration.
The most popular shape was the pear-shape.

BELLOWS PARTS   Fig.327

Leather loop. This sometimes went
around the front handle and through
a hole in the back handle.

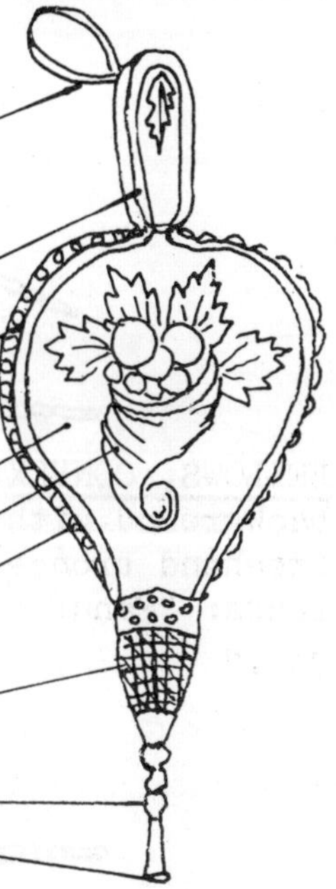

Handle

Leather sides (reed supports inside)

Face

Design

Brass stud

Hinge (hand-woven leather)

Brass nozzle (or nose)

Orifice

Hole for loop

Brush stroke design

Orifice

Back

Brass nozzle (hand turned)
Also called the pip

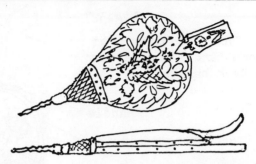

BELLOWS, CONVEX. Connecticut. Mid-1800's. Deep green background with two gold-leaf cornucopias containing freehand bronze fruit, leaves, and border. Label on back reads: "Manufactured by Bateman & Stevens Salem Bridge Con." Fig.328

BELLOWS, CONVEX. Connecticut. 1840-1850's. 17 1/2" x 7 1/4". Yellow background with two deep bronze leaves in the center. Silver bronze leaves, fruit, and red berries make up the rest of the design. Bateman & Stevens label in the back orifice. Fig.329

BELLOWS, FLAT FACE. Sometimes called "flat iron" or "trivet." From the Midlands, England, Early 1800's. 17 3/4" x 8". Gold-leaf basket and flowers with freehand bronze fruit and fill-ins on a green background. Fig.330

BELLOWS. England. 1790-1810. 13" x
5 1/4". Indian work, oriental style
painting in gold leaf with red background on a flat back. Also found on
white, green, or black background.
                              Fig.331

BELLOWS, LONG AND NARROW. Also called "hearth bellows." Boston. 1836-
1850. 12" x 4 3/4". Japanned in
fancy oriental style, done in metal
leaf on a red background. Possibly
by Drew and Hixon who advertised in
the Boston papers.   Fig.332

BELLOWS, PAGODA BACK. Possibly Birmingham, England. 1800-1810. 13"
x 5 1/4". Japanned on a dark brown
background with freehand bronze and
gold leaf.   Fig.333

BELLOWS, PEAR-SHAPED. Birmingham,
England. 14" x 5 1/2". A popular
shape, painted lilies-of-the-valley
design, possibly by William Jackson.
Cream background. Papier-mâché.
                              Fig.334

BELLOWS, TURTLEBACK. Boston, Albany, Philadelphia, and
Connecticut. Late 18th and early 19th centuries.
18 1/2" x 8 1/2". Stenciled and freehand bronzed.These
bellows were found with all color backgrounds except
black. Some were smoked.   Fig.335

BRIDE'S BOXES

Bride's boxes from Austria, Bavaria, the Palatinate,
Scandinavia and Switzerland, were brought to Pennsylvania by immigrants in the 17th and 18th centuries. A
supplement to the bride's chest, they were handsomely
decorated, with much freedom, and often were referred
to as "gift," "hat," or "dressing" boxes. In some
sections of Europe they were also called "chip" boxes.
The top usually shows a picture with a motto, romantic
or practical, in old German lettering. The gay design
along the side runs free, without panel interruption.
From 6" to 26" long, average size.

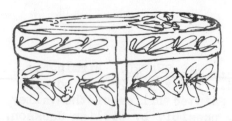

BRIDE'S BOXES. Germany. Late 1700's. 24" long, 4"
deep. Elaborately decorated in color.   Fig.336

BRIDE'S BOX. Germany. Top bedecked with soldier in
red, and floral wreaths. Green, red, and black floral
design on side. 18" long by 6" deep.   Fig.337

BRIDE'S BOX. Germany. Late 18th
century. 14 1/2" long x 6" high,
10 1/2" wide. Dark green background
with yellow, red, and green tulip
design.   Fig.338

BRIDE'S BOXES, AMERICAN. BERKS COUNTY

Henry or Heinrich Bucher decorated oval and rectangular
boxes with black backgrounds and a variety of peculiar
tulips -- closed, partly open, in bud, or full bloom, in
red and yellow. His boxes are like the imported bride's
boxes in shape and construction, but are not fastened
together with thongs or withes. Berks County boxes were
shaved to paper thinness where they overlapped, then
glued together. Another feature: the flowers on the side
of the cover did not match the ones on the side of the
box.

BRIDE'S BOX. An H. Bucher piece. Approximately 15" long
and 5" deep. Cream band border on top, the rest the
usual red and yellow tulips with green foliage on a black
background.   Fig.339

BRIDE'S BOX. Also called a "dressing" box. Pennsylvania. 14 1/2" x 8" x 10 1/2". Arched lid. Was locally
painted in gay colors.   Fig.340

BRIDE'S BOX. Germany. Late 18th
century. 14 1/2" x 8" x 10 1/2".
On a dark green background, with
yellow, red, and green tulip design.
                                Fig.341

CANDLE BOX. Pennsylvania. Circa
1800. 16" x 10" x 7". Boldly
painted in Pennsylvania country
style in red, green, and brown on
yellow background. Has a sliding
top. Miscalled a "knife" box.

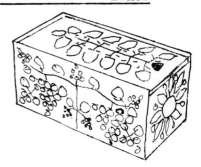

Fig.342

CHAIRMAKER'S or JOINER'S BOX. Massachusetts.   1850.
10" x 5" x 3 7/8".   Decorated with typical stencil units
used by a chair decorator.   Fig.343

HOUSE-TYPE BOX. Pennsylvania. Mid-
1800's. 4" long, 2" wide, and
3 1/4" deep. Tulips are red, white,
and green on yellow background.
These were very popular and were
frequently done in water color.
Floral top was probably a transfer.
See "decalcomanie" in the Vocabulary.   Fig.344

JEWELRY BOX. England. Circa 1798.
10" x 5" x 3". Design done in India
ink on a natural wood box, called
"penwork." See also Fig.359.
                              Fig.345

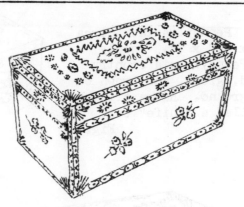

<u>NEW HAMPSHIRE BOX</u>. So-called because of its origin.
23" long, 12" wide, and 8" high. Stenciled with bronze
powders in the center top; also stenciled with paint.
Rather thick red, blue, and white daisies and flower
sprays. After 1850.   Fig.346

<u>RANSOM COOK'S BOX</u>. An excellent
example of Mr. Cook's work. New
York. Circa 1843. 12" x 6" x 6".
Stenciled on black.   Fig.347

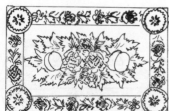

Top of Ransom Cook's box, Fig.347A

SEWING BOX. England. Found in the London market.
Circa 1815. 8" x 6" x 9 1/2". A platform-top regency
box with drawers. The flower painting inside and out
on this yellow box is so-called "Chippendale" painting
and is exceptionally beautiful.   Fig.348

TEA BOX. England. Circa 1860.
5 1/2" x 4 1/4" x 3 1/4". Lacquer-
ed box, all metal-leaf oriental design. The inside has two sections,
one for green tea, the other for
black.   Fig.349

TEA BOX, OVAL. Midlands, England.
Circa 1800. 6 1/2" x 4 3/4" x 3 1/2".
Painted country scene on yellow
background. Hinge in back, lock in
front.   Fig.350

TRINKET BOX. Europe and Pennsylvania import. 1790-1850. 4 1/2" x
2 1/4" x 3". Made of a thin sheet
of wood which has been steamed or
soaked in hot water, then bent around
a block and neatly bound with split
willow or thongs. Some are fastened with small wooden pegs, hence the
name "bent wood" box.   Fig.351

BRUSHES

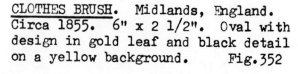

CLOTHES BRUSH. Midlands, England. Circa 1855. 6" x 2 1/2". Oval with design in gold leaf and black detail on a yellow background.   Fig.352

CLOTHES BRUSH. Pennsylvania. Circa 1840. 8 1/2" x 3". A white flower with alizarin wash and green leaves on a cream colored background.
Fig.353

CRUMBER BRUSH. Midlands, England. 1800's. Gold leaf flower design, with freehand bronze leaves and black details on a yellow background. Red sides and handle. Black stripes.
Fig.354

HEARTH BRUSH. Pennsylvania. Circa 1800's. 12" long. Design: white flowers and green leaves on a cream background. Many stripes. Fig.355

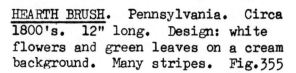

HEARTH BRUSH. Midlands, England. 1815. 28 1/2" overall. A mahogany grained background, many gold leaf borders. One section is gold leaf with freehand bronze and painting. Has a fine Sheraton feeling.
Fig.356

BUCKETS

UTILITY BUCKET or PAIL. (A vessel
carried by hand.) Pennsylvania.
1800's. 10" high and 8" in diameter.
Pennsylvania Dutch motifs and distelfink.   Fig.357

WATER BUCKET. With handle. Pennsylvania. Circa 1825. 10" high, 11"
in diameter. Gayly colored flowers
and leaves with brushstroke border
above and below. Stained background.
                              Fig.358

CANDLE SHIELD. England. Popular
from 1793-1804. 7" wide by 10 1/2"
high. Penwork design. See also
Fig.345.   Fig.359

CORNICE BOARDS

These were found from Main to South Carolina from 1790-
1850. They served as "dress-up" tops for Venetian
blinds and were 7" to 8 1/2" high, and up to 45" long.
Usually stenciled on black or green backgrounds, more
rarely found on yellow ochre or red grounds.

The Venetian blinds, sometimes in the same color, were
drawn up under the cornices. These were imported into
America as early as 1767, and by the middle of 1770 were
being made here. After 1840 they were quite common.

CORNICE BOARD. New York. 1817-1843. 8 1/2" x 39 1/2".
Background green except for the two rectangles which
are black and stenciled. Center motif gold-leaf basket
with beautifully stenciled fruit. Gold-leaf cornucopias, with stenciled fruit and flowers, the rest freehand bronze.   Fig.360

CORNICE BOARD. New York. Circa 1814. 8" x 44 1/2"
A Hudson River stenciled scene enclosed in a broad
stripe, with gold leaf ends. Black backgrounds.

Fig.361

CORNICE BOARD. Long Island, New York. Circa 1810.
8" x 40". Stenciled in shades of bronze on a green
background. Gold leaf units at the ends and in the
center. Bamboo half-rounds border the design. This
cornice shows the Venetian blind in position. Fig.362

CORNICE BOARD. New York. Circa 1834. 8 1/4" x 39 1/2".
Shaped board with end pieces and three gold-leaf units.
The main section is stenciled with fruit and flowers,
and bamboo framed. Green background with black panels.
Fig.363

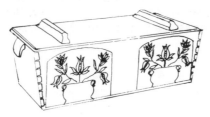

DOUGH TROUGH. Pennsylvania. Circa 1792. Vermilion
front board with white panels. Design in green, red,
and brown leaves. Dovetailed ends. Attributed to
Christian Seltzer, 1747-1831, of Lebanon County.
Fig.364

FIREBOARD. Also called a "chimney" board. 45" x 38".
18th and 19th centuries. An itinerant painter may
have done this for a meal. Painted in perspective to
look like tile facing. The vase is almost a stock
pattern. It varied little. Border of trees. Fig.365

FIREBOARD. New England. 1820-1825. 42" x 32". Stenciled in red, green, and black with units similar to those used by Moses Eaton on walls accredited to him.
Fig.366

FRAMES

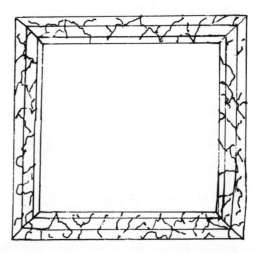

FRAME. Massachusetts. Circa 1791. Approximately
22 1/2" x 16 1/2". Black marbleizing on an ivory ground.
Bolection molded.   Fig.367

FRAME. New England, possibly Massachusetts. Circa
1840. 7 1/8" x 5 1/2". Design stenciled in one shade
of bronze. The eagle was a popular patriotic motif.
                                                    Fig.368

FRAME. Kutztown, Pennsylvania.
Mid-1800's. 13 1/2" x 9 3/4".
Dots, scrolls, rick-rack, lines
and daisies, painted in white,
red, yellow, and blue. Fig.369

FRAME. Pennsylvania. Early 19th
century. 18" x 16". Two-toned
graining, which was done all over
New England.   Fig.370

LEHN WARE

(See Joseph Lehn under "Painters and Craftsmen")

BUCKET. With cover. Clay, Pennsylvania. Circa 1860. 10" high. A pinkish background with pussy willow border pattern. Lehn's favorite strawberry pattern on top.

Fig.371

 EGG CUP. Pennsylvania. 1860-1886. 3 1/2" tall. Very colorfully done in pink, red, blue, and green.

Fig.372

 URN-SHAPED CUP. Pennsylvania. Circa 1875. 4". The edge of the foot is blue with a green stripe, then a red stem. Green stripe under the pink bowl and a red border at top.

Fig.373

 SAFFRON BOX. Pennsylvania. 1860-1886. 5 1/2" tall. Lehn seems to have had a set formula for these boxes and urn cups. Foot dark blue, then a green stripe, a red stem, another green stripe, a pink bowl, and finally a bright red border. The lid has a dark blue knob and the strawberry design. Fig.374

<u>TUB</u>. Pennsylvania. 1860-1886. 8"
high, 16" in diameter. Pink mottling
over a yellow ground, with pussy willow borders.   Fig.375

<u>PAINTED PANEL</u>. From the walls of a
drawing room on a Mississippi River
boat. 1830.   Fig.376

<u>SCHIMMEL BIRDS</u>

(See <u>William Schimmel</u> under "Painters and Craftsmen.")

<u>EAGLE</u>. Pennsylvania. Circa 1860. 18 1/2" with 29"
wingspread. Carved and polychromed by William Schimmel.
                                                Fig.377

PARROT. Pennsylvania. Circa 1865. 10 1/4". Carved and painted by William Schimmel. Done in many bright colors.   Fig.378

SIGN. American. 18th and 19th centuries. Used by tradesmen to advertise their wares and places of business, taverns, and for collecting tolls. This shape was popular from 1749-1826.   Fig.379

CLOCKS

MANTEL OR SHELF CLOCKS

The earliest American shelf clock was the type known as
the Massachusetts or "half" clock. It was made by the
Willards and others after the Revolutionary War. Simon
Willard is believed to have given up the manufacture of
his banjo clock, but Aaron and others continued manufacturing them into the first quarter of the 19th century.

The largest number and variety of shelf clocks were
produced by Connecticut makers. By 1808 Eli Terry had
made his first 34-hour, wood, shelf clock. By 1818 he
had developed the pillar-and-scroll clock which survived until 1830. There were many others who copied
his pillar-and-scroll clock.

ACORN CLOCK. Connecticut. 1825-
1845. 24" high. Reverse scenic
painting on glass.   Fig.380

ACORN CLOCK. Connecticut. Circa
1845. 24 1/2" high. Reverse
scenic painting on glass. Decoration on clock dial.   Fig.381

BEEHIVE CLOCK. Bristol, Connecticut. 1850-1860. Transfer print
with painting in black. A very
popular model. Similar to a "lancet" clock, which was English, and
so called because the shape of the
top resembled the surgeon's lancet.
In vogue from 1800-1850. Top sug-
gestive of the Gothic arch. Fig.382

GOTHIC or CATHEDRAL CLOCK. Bristol,
Connecticut. 1830-1835. 15" high.
Tablet design is stenciled and frosted. Possibly designed by Elias Ingraham who designed the steeple
clock about this time. This clock
has been whittled from one piece
of wood.   Fig.383

GOTHIC DOUBLE-STEEPLE CLOCK. Bristol, Connecticut. 1843-1848. 19"
to 20" high. Two tablets of stenciled and frosted glass. Sometimes
called a "double decker."   Fig.384

GOTHIC or RIPPLED STEEPLE CLOCK.
Connecticut. 1842-1848. Engraved
tablet depicts a balloon ascending.
Fig. 385

MANTEL CLOCK. A development of
Terry. Three panels. 37" high.
Made by Barnes, Bartholomew & Co.,
Bristol, Connecticut. 1830-1840.
Reverse painting: country scenes on
center tablet and lower door. Side
columns gilded.   Fig. 386

MANTEL CLOCK. Terry style. Bristol, Connecticut. Circa 1835. 30"
tall. Mezzotint print on the glass
tablet is of St. Luke's Church in
New York. Stenciled borders and
two cyma curves form the stenciled
top section. Half columns are stenciled.   Fig. 387

MANTEL CLOCK. Plymouth, Connecticut. 1815-1835. By Seth Thomas in
the Terry style. Stenciled fruit
and flowers on top and on half columns. Tablet has painting of large
country house, tree, and stenciled
border. Stenciled half columns.
Fig.388

MANTEL CLOCK. Simple shelf type.
After 1837. 11" x 7". A popular
clock. Transfer scene is back-
painted.   Fig.389

METAL CLOCK. Connecticut. Circa
1860. 12" high. Pearl shell.
Metal-leaf scrolls and painted flowers make up the design.   Fig.390

OGEE CLOCK. 1869. 25" x 16 1/2".
Transfer design around coat-of-arms.
This clock appeared around 1825, at
first with wooden movements; after
1837, with brass movements. After
1850 many mezzotints were found on
this type clock.   Fig.391

PAPIER-MÂCHE CLOCK. Litchfield,
Connecticut. 1850-1854. 18" high.
Gold-leaf scroll work with fine
Chippendale painting. Birds and
flowers most likely done by pro-
fessionals such as an English ar-
tist at the Litchfield plant.
See also page 303.   Fig.392

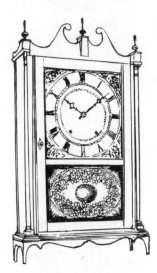

PILLAR AND SCROLL CLOCK. Plymouth,
Connecticut. 1794-1818. Made by
Eli Terry & Son. Tablet has gold-
leaf border with fine painting of
roses.   Fig.393

PILLAR AND SCROLL CLOCK. Plymouth,
Connecticut. Circa 1816. Made by
Eli Terry. Gold leaf border around
floral design on reverse side of
glass. The escapement on the glass
and the pendulum hole off-center were
found on the early Terry clocks.
                             Fig.394

PILLAR AND SCROLL CLOCK. Plymouth
and Watertown, Connecticut. 1823-
1830. By J. Bishop and L. Bradley.
Tablet has painted architectural
scene. A good copy of a Terry-type
clock. Note that there is no pendulum hole.   Fig.395

The Willard brothers, who were famous
for their banjo clocks, were the
first to make clocks with glass
fronts, top and bottom, an idea
that was soon copied.

WILLARD CLOCK. Boston. From 1802
on. 35" high, 16" wide, and 6"
deep. Made by Aaron Willard. Lower glass painted with a pastoral
scene, floral stencil border, also
around dial. Acorn finial and
bracket feet. Willard clocks are
known for their fine paintings.
                                 Fig.396

WILLARD CLOCK. Roxbury, Massachusetts. From 1802. 35" high. Made
by Aaron Willard. Broken pediment
top cresting. The bottom has a
heavy rounded piece such as is found
on empire-style furniture of the
period, and has feet. Leaf and
daisy pattern is stenciled around
dial and lower tablet on the reverse side of the glass along with
a painting of a wayside scene in the
country.   Fig.397

WILLARD-STYLE MANTEL CLOCK. Boston.
Circa 1810. Four gold-leaf lyres
around the dial; lower tablet a
painting of Mt. Vernon, with gold
leaf around it. Note the resemblance
to the Terry style in the scroll top.
Fig.398

STANDING CLOCKS

The colloquial term -- "grandfather clock" -- is so
familiar that it is preferred to such terms as "long,"
"tall," or "hall," which are also used. The origin of
the name "grandfather clock" is said to come from a
song written in 1880. They were made from 1690 to
1860. We are listing them as "tall" clocks.

TALL CASE CLOCK. England. Circa
1720. 7' 6 1/4" tall. Silvered
dial. Signed "Isaac Rogers, London." Japanned green background.
Design: chinoiserie in gold leaf.
(At left) Fig.399

TALL CASE CLOCK. Pennsylvania.
Circa 1830. Flat top, arched dial,
profusely decorated on a pale red
background.   (At right) Fig.400

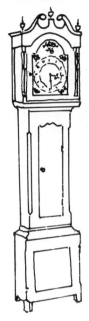

TALL CASE CLOCK. American. Circa 1820-1830. From 90" to 108" tall. Arched dial with painted units. Three brass finials.   Fig.401

TALL CASE CLOCK. Possibly Boston or New York. Early 19th century. Stenciled and painted case. Signed at bottom: "R. Cole, painter." Just over 7' tall. Grained pine case. Negative stencil of deer outside arched dial. Small painted scene on dial. Waist has stenciled diamond and four corner units. Fruit stencil in bottom diamond. Plinth stenciled with leaves. Broken pediment has stenciled daisies.   Fig.402

The term "grandmother clock" is also American terminology. It is a small floor clock in the grandfather form, the case in three parts -- the hood above, the base below, and the waist between, with a door.

GRANDMOTHER CLOCK. Also called a "small grandfather" or "dwarf" clock. Made by Joshua Wilder, Hingham, Massachusetts. Born 1786, died 1860. He made only the working parts while local cabinet makers made the cases. No exact height is given for these clocks. This one is 44 1/2" high and has a painted dial of fruit. Another one is 53 1/4" high and has an 8" dial.   Fig.403

WALL CLOCKS

The earliest wall clock was the "wag-on-the-wall." Simon
Willard started to make wall clocks in 1783. He developed the banjo clock in 1802. Most of the Willard clocks
were made with a throat tablet. In later models, mahogany panels were used because the hand-painted tablets
were difficult to produce. After 1842, a late banjo-type
clock was made with a plain wood case.

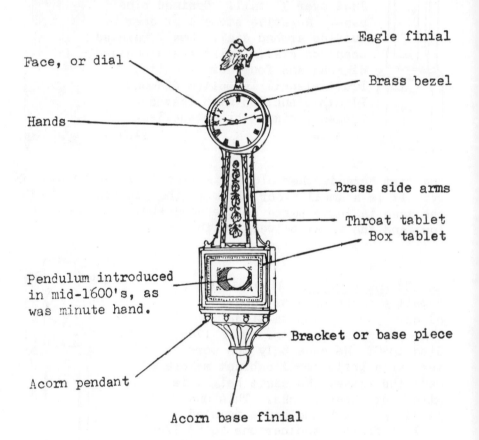

Eagle finial

Face, or dial

Brass bezel

Hands

Brass side arms

Throat tablet
Box tablet

Pendulum introduced
in mid-1600's, as
was minute hand.

Bracket or base piece

Acorn pendant

Acorn base finial

BANJO CLOCK.

Figure 404

BANJO CLOCK. Massachusetts. Circa
1815. 36". Aaron Willard. A mythological subject painted on the box
tablet. Both throat and box tablets
are done in reverse painting. Acorn
finial.   Fig.405

BANJO CLOCK. Roxbury, Massachusetts.
Circa 1812. 33" high. A good example
of Simon Willard's 8-day timepiece.
The tablet has gold-leaf borders, the
throat has gold-leaf lattice work or
so-called crosshatching design, done
by Penniman.   Fig.406

BANJO CLOCK. More often called a timepiece rather than a clock. Simon Willard. Mahogany case. Brass sidearms
and brass bezel case with painted
throat and base tablet. Throat design gold leaf, oak leaves, and acorns,
backed with a white paint. Tablet design, blue paint and gold leaf units
backed, too, with white paint.
                                 Fig.407

TWO BANJO CLOCKS. Both are Simon
Willard Presentation Timepieces.
Roxbury, Massachusetts. Circa 1810-
1828. Only the presentation pieces
had the eagle finial. Carved base.
The brass sidearms of the timepiece
on the left are of unusual design.
Throat and tablets have etched gold-
leaf designs. 43" high. The one on
the right might possibly have been
decorated by J. R. Penniman. Fig.408

CURTIS CLOCK. Concord, Massachusetts
and Burlington, Vermont. 1810-1830.
45" high. Sometimes called a "Girandole Clock." Reverse painting of an
eagle on the throat and a mythological subject on the convex tablet.
Considered the most beautiful American clock. Fine carved base piece
with gold balls around the convex
glass tablet. By Lemuel Curtis.
Fig.409

CURTIS CLOCK. Concord, Massachusetts
and Burlington, Vermont. 1810-1830.
45" high. By Lemuel Curtis. Reverse
painting of ships on convex glass
tablet. Eagle design on throat.
Spread eagle finial and carved base
piece.   Fig.410

LOOKING-GLASS CLOCK. Also called "New
Hampshire Looking-Glass Clock." 1820-
1840. 26" x 14" x 4". Stenciled around
the clock face. Attributed to Ben Mor-
ril, Boscawen, N.H. Produced by several makers, mostly in New Hampshire,
hence the name.   Fig.411

LOOKING-GLASS CLOCK. Hew Hampshire
and Massachusetts. 1825-1830. 32"
x 15". Unusual architectural top.
Four rosettes in the corner. Baluster columns. Four units stenciled
around the dial. Frame black, with
gold-leaf turnings. Sometimes called a "New Hampshire Mirror Clock."
                              Fig.412

LYRE CLOCK. Massachusetts. 1820-1840.
40 1/2" tall. Aaron Willard design.
Fleur-de-lis finial, acorn base piece.
Stenciled behind the carved lyre.
Gold-leaf border on tablet with paint-
ed seascape.   Fig.413

LYRE CLOCK. Boston. 1800-1820.
36 1/2". Stenciled on the glass
within the carved lyre front. Naval
scene in reverse glass painting. Made
by Swain and Dyer.   Fig.414

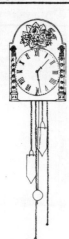

WAG-ON-THE-WALL CLOCK. Pennsylvania.
1783. 9 1/2" x 14". Arched dial wall
clock consisting of painted face and
works waiting for a tall case. Design:
large painted flowers and two columns
in bright colors.   Fig.415

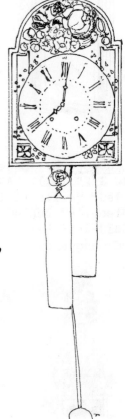

WAG-ON-THE-WALL CLOCK. Pennsylvania.
Early 1800's. Arched dial, 10" x
13 1/2", gayly painted in brilliant
red, blue, yellow, and green. A rose,
other flowers, strawberries, and
columns make up the design. Fig.416

LOOKING GLASSES

LOOKING GLASSES OR MIRRORS

The term "mirror" referred to any polished surface, either
metal or glass, used to reflect objects. A distinction
was made during the seventeenth and eighteenth centuries
between the use of "mirror" and "looking glass." Judging
from inventories and advertisements, the word "mirror"
was used when referring to those with convex glass (the
term "dished" was also used for the curved glass), and
"looking glass" when referring to the rest. The terms
include both glass and frame, but the particular style
is determined by the shape of the frame. We have used
the term "looking glass" instead of "mirror" because a
looking glass is framed, not just a piece to reflect an
image.

ARCHITECTURAL LOOKING GLASSES

These are also called "tabernacle" or "Sheraton looking
glasses," 1780-1820, so called because of their construction. They have a flat cornice, or projection, at
the top, usually supporting nine to twenty-two gold-leaf
pendant balls or acorns. The cornice is supported by
columns which are single- or double-reeded, fluted or
plain, with or without capitals. Gold-leaf and mahogany frames sometimes have a solid frieze panel with a
carved decoration, and, below it, an eglomise panel, a
reverse painted landscape or patriotic symbol, a reverse painting of a naval engagement or a vase of flowers or fruit, also in reverse. The more elaborate Sheraton looking glasses of the Hudson River Valley School
of Painting (1790-1820) may be distinguished by the
cresting on the cornice, festoons of gold leaf balls,
and eglomise panels featuring urns of flowers and wheat
ears. Sometimes they are topped by a high eagle finial.

ARCHITECTURAL LOOKING GLASS

Parts:
1. Cornice
2. Pendant gold-leaf balls
3. Corbel
4. Applied ornamental design
5. Églomisé panel
6. Capital
7. Column
8. Looking glass
9. Corner block
10. Porcelain knobs

Fig. 417

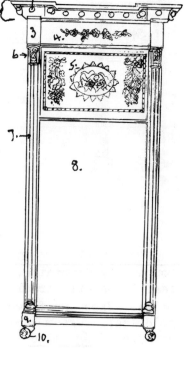

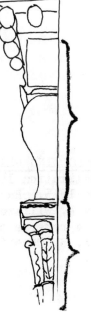

Side view of corbel, no. 3

Side view of capital, no. 6

Fig. 417A

ARCHITECTURAL LOOKING GLASS. Pennsylvania. Early 19th century. A
rural type, with painting of hearts
in red, yellow, and green on the glass
panel. The frame is grained.

Fig.418

ARCHITECTURAL LOOKING GLASS. Portsmouth, New Hampshire. 1812. Gold-
leaf frame with traditional gold-leaf
balls. Vase and flowers are etched
gold leaf. Cream background. Good
example of églomisé tablet. Fig.419

ARCHITECTURAL LOOKING GLASS. Miscalled a "Constitution looking glass."
Boston. Circa 1815. Has double columns. Made by A. Willard and Nolen.
The design is a reverse painting on
glass of the S. S. Constitution and
the Guerrière.   Fig.420

ARCHITECTURAL LOOKING GLASS. Sheraton type. Albany, New York. Circa 1790-1810. A composition ornament above the crest is linked by 24 gold-leaf balls. The panel is etched gold leaf, églomisé tablet.   Fig.421

ARCHITECTURAL LOOKING GLASS. American. Circa 1815. Double columns with insets of glass, done in the églomisé style, possibly by John R. Penniman. The picture is a scene in gold leaf, with red, blue, and cream painting on the back.   Fig.422

ARCHITECTURAL LOOKING GLASS. Boston. 1800-1810. 26" x 14". Thought to be done by Cermenati and Monfrino. The tablet has a memorial urn with George Washington's name on it and flags on either side. Under the cornice there is an unusual ornamental molding.   Fig.423

ARCHITECTURAL LOOKING GLASS. Vicinity
of Pennsylvania. Circa 1796., Attractive small gold-leaf balls. Églomisé
tablet. Compo design on columns and
below cornice are indication of an
early piece.   Fig.424

COUNTRY LOOKING GLASS. New
England. Circa 1840. Black
frame with four rosettes in
the corner blocks. Attract-
ively stenciled.   Fig.425

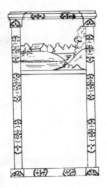

COUNTRY LOOKING GLASS. American.
Circa 1850. 21 1/2" x 11 3/4".
Simple painted scene on the glass
panel. The concave black frame is
stenciled.   Fig.426

COUNTRY LOOKING GLASS.
American. 1850. 19" x
12". Possibly made by a
chair decorator. Black,
with typical chair sten-
ciling. A flat frame
with four corner blocks.
                    Fig.427

COUNTRY LOOKING GLASS. Pennsylvania. Circa 1830. 18 1/2"
high by 15" wide. Large units
stenciled on a black (sides)
and white background. Four
corner blocks done with the
same unit.   Fig.428

COURTING MIRROR
(Or "Looking Glass in a Box")

Details:
1. Angular crest
2. Stylized floral painting
3. Crossette frame
4. Narrow, half-round molding
5. Glass border inset
6. Concave molding
7. Looking glass
8. Wooden box

Size: 21" x 9 1/2"

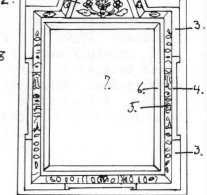

Fig.429

It was thought that the courting mirrors, found in great
numbers in seaport towns from New Hampshire to Delaware,
were of Chinese origin, and according to tradition, a
customary courting gift. In recent research by Judith
Coolidge Hughes (Antiques Magazine, July 1962 and June
1966) it has been established that the courting mirror
was made in the Dutch-influenced countries of northern
Europe, Holland, North Germany, and Denmark, from 1700
to 1810. The frames resemble the angular frames and
chairs of the Flemish and Dutch of this period.

From tests made at Winterthur it has been determined that
the wood of many of these mirrors is Scotch pine, which
is found in these countries, not in the Orient. Although
usually worn off, the inner moldings were originally covered with Dutch metal leaf. The glass was not beveled
and the glass painting in the crest was generally stylized
flowers or fruit, sometimes landscapes and figures. These
mirrors came in one-board boxes with sliding covers, and
were held in place with wooden pegs. The box was usually
stained or painted earth-red, green, or brown. Very
often the looking glass was not separated from the box,
but hung with it. There were three popular types:

1. Those with narrow, half round, and fillet moldings,
an inner concave molding, crossettes, and floral painting
in the crest, and glass border inserts. See Fig.429.

2. Wide, half-round, and fillet moldings, inner concave
molding, crossettes, and floral painting on glass in crest,
but with no glass border inserts. See Fig.430.

3. Narrow reeded moldings, the inner one convex, straight
sides and marbleized glass borders. See Fig. 431 and 432.

Fig.430

COURTING MIRROR. Imported. 18th century. 21" x 9 1/2". Floral design
on the crest; borders marbleized.
                                    Fig.431

COURTING MIRROR. Imported. 18th
century. 21" x 9 1/2". The borders
are marbleized glass. There is a
floral design on the crest, with
Dutch metal on the narrow molding.
                                    Fig.432

EMPIRE LOOKING GLASSES

The Empire looking glass was also known as the "American
empire" or "baluster looking glass." 1810-1840. It had
no projecting cornice, but the columns of the architectural looking glass remained. These were half-round pilasters in various styles, spirally reeded, acanthus carved,
vase and ring, or vase and cylinder. The pilasters were
turned and carved, then split down the center and applied
to the four sides of the plain wooden frame. They were
finished as plain wood, partially gilded and/or ebonized.
Brass rosettes or other motifs were usually attached to
the square corner blocks. The nearly square glass panel
in the upper part was decorated with a reverse glass
painting of a landscape, naval engagement or urn of fruit
or flowers in color.

EMPIRE (NON-ARCHITECTURAL) LOOKING
GLASS. Circa 1830. Gilded columns
with applied designs. Painted glass
panel with stenciled border. Four
rosettes at corners.   Fig.433

EMPIRE LOOKING GLASS. New England.
Circa 1830. 21" x 11". Baluster
columns, split, and four corner blocks
with rosettes. Gold-leaf turnings
and black sections. Tablet has stenciled border with a painted country
scene.   Fig.434

EMPIRE LOOKING GLASS. New England.
Circa 1830. 21" x 12". Eagles on
the columns made of compo and gold-
leafed. Painted fruit scene on tablet, with gold-leaf and paint-stip-
pled border.   Fig.435

HEPPLEWHITE LOOKING GLASS. England.
1790. An oblong looking glass with
broken pediment cresting and valenced
apron. Its églomisé panel and ornate
detailed work, such as wheat ears
and flowers on wire stems, and Adam-
esque urn, are similar to those of the
Hudson Valley or New York Sheraton
looking glasses.   Fig.436

QUEEN ANNE LOOKING GLASS. New York.
Mid-18th century. A transitional
type with heavily scrolled crest;
japanned with gold-leaf decoration,
combining oriental figures, architecture, diaper patterns, and shell
motifs.   Fig.437

OVERMANTEL LOOKING GLASS. Also called "chimney looking
glass" or "Sheraton overmantel mirror." A horizontal looking glass designed to correspond to the paneling of the
chimney breast. It was usually made and designed in three
sections of glass, with églomisé panels or other forms of
ornamentation, in accord with the frame and period. 1780-
1820.   Fig.438

FURNITURE

COUNTRY BEDROOM FURNITURE

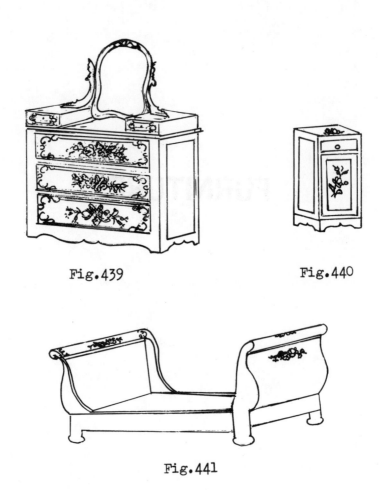

Fig.439   Fig.440

Fig.441

COUNTRY BEDROOM FURNITURE. New England. 1830-1850.
Simple suites such as these were turned out for cottages
and country places. On a cream background, flower sprays
of many colors were painted and banded. This type furniture was also found with grained backgrounds and scroll
designs, with wide striping.   Fig.439, 440, and 441

CHAIRS

Adam chairs. England. 1760-1780. Usually in soft colors, with medallions, Adam urn, ribbons, Greek stylized honeysuckle, husks, feathers, swags, fans, **egg-and-dart** borders, and **acanthus leaves.**

ADAM CHAIR. England. Circa 1760. Balusters, apron, and front legs decorated with garlands of flowers and leaves. Green chair with H **stretcher.**   Fig.442

ADAM-HEPPLEWHITE CHAIR. Since it is practically impossible to draw a sharp line between period designs of furniture makers, because various pattern books were available to them, we use the term "Adam-Hepplewhite" loosely. This one is English. 1785-1800. Oval back with bow-knots, leaves, rosebuds, brown feathers, urns, and ribbons.
                                    Fig.443

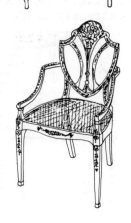

ADAM-HEPPLEWHITE CHAIR. England. Circa 1790. Painted satinwood cane seat, shield back with fine flower decoration all over this delicate chair.   Fig.444

BALTIMORE CHAIR

The Baltimore or so-called "southern" chair is of the
American Empire period, circa 1815-1840. It was at the
height of its popularity around 1825. They were made in
Baltimore, also in other parts of Maryland, Washington,
D.C., Winchester and Alexandria, Virginia. They should
not be confused with the Baltimore furniture of an earlier
period, which was lighter and had greater elegance.

The "southern chair" has a wide, deep top rail (slat), a
seat with a front roll, heavy seat sides and turned legs.
The stiles curve down into the seat. Usually there is a
narrow middle slat, but some, from Winchester, resemble
the folding bronze chairs found in Egypt in the way the
back legs join the stiles and seat in a round, wheel-like
hinge. They had cane, rush, and sometimes plank seats.

They were painted chairs: white, soft green, and other
light colors, as well as dark shades, black, and grained.
The decoration was highly ornamental, with classical motifs, and often a small scene in an oval on the top rail,
borrowed probably from the earlier Baltimore chairs of
the Sheraton period.

Many stripes and bandings were a prominent feature of this
chair. It had straight front legs with large, often gilded turnings, thick wedge-shaped seat sides called "elbows"
and deep seats. The back cant was compensated for by the
backward and downward thrust of the back legs. They are
extremely comfortable chairs.

BALTIMORE CHAIR. Painted. Sheraton
influence. Circa 1805. Made by John
and Hugh Finlay whose period was 1799-
1833. The Carrol family estates are
painted on the slat while the rest of
the chair is decorated with gold-leaf
and painted motifs. Cane seat and
tapered legs. Typical Baltimore
piece.   Fig.445

BALTIMORE CHAIR. Circa 1820. Rolled
top slat, freehand bronze design with
color washes, all else solid bronzing. Black chair with a so-called
"upside down Queen Anne vase." Cane
seat.   Fig.446

BALTIMORE CHAIR. Circa 1830. Cane
seat with a scenic stenciled design
on a black background. "Elbows" are
found on most so-called "Southern"
chairs.   Fig.447

BALTIMORE CHAIR. 1830-1835. Narrow
back slat, broad slat top. Cane
seat. Freehand bronze painting and
gold turnings.   Fig.448

BALTIMORE CHAIR. Circa 1810-1825.
Raked back and rear legs are joined
to resemble the folding bronze chairs
found in Egypt. A gold-leaf decoration imitates hinges; sometimes
thought of as "elbows." Front legs
are fluted. Painted flowers and gold-
leaf scrolls on slat and seat roll.
Cane seat.   Fig.449

BALTIMORE CHAIR. Circa 1825. Classical gold-leaf design on dark brown.
almost black, background. A child's
                                    Fig.450

BOSS TWEED CHAIR. New York. Named for
William Marcy Tweed, Chairmaker, 1823-
1878. Also called a "Victorian" chair
of the eara around 1845. Oval cane
seat; shield-type back, profusely decorated with metal-leaf scrolls, pearl
shell, and flower painting.   Fig.451

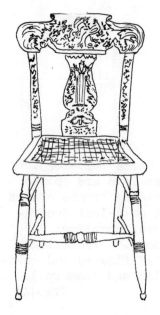

FIDDLEBACK CHAIR. Massachusetts.
Circa 1845. Also called a "fancy
roll-top" chair. Stenciled by W. P.
Eaton on a black background. Cane
seat. Chair named for the shape of
its splat.   Fig.452

FIDDLEBACK CHAIR. New York. Circa
1845. Sometimes mistakenly called a
"banister-back" chair. Scenic stencil on slat, scroll stencil on
splat. By Cutting and Morrill. Cane
seat, grained background.   Fig.453

DIRECTOIRE FURNITURE, so-called because it was made in
France circa 1795-1799, a period in which the executive
power in that country was held by a body called the "Directoire," frequently called "Directory" in English. It
is a transitional style, between Louis XVI and Empire,
and not easily distinguishable from the latter.

The AMERICAN DIRECTORY STYLE of furniture, 1805-1815, was
an import from France, but it also shows a strong English
Sheraton influence. It leads directly into the Empire
style. However, evidence of the Directory style is notice-
able as late as 1840.

The EMPIRE STYLE originated in France under Napoleon, 1804
1815. It uses classical and oriental motifs, long curving
lines, and carving and ornamentation in brass and ivory.

The AMERICAN EMPIRE STYLE was developed as early as 1805
and lasted until 1840, when the Victorian period took over.
Chairs of the Empire period are said to be the best designed of that period. It was also an era of fine stenciling, and this is seen to advantage on pianos. Much of the
stenciling on the piano cases was done directly on the
rosewood or mahogany, and embellished further with gold-
leaf decoration. See Fig.550.

Duncan Phyfe, 1768-1854, American master of the FEDERAL
STYLE, worked in a modified Directory-Empire style, which

degenerated after 1820. The designation "Federal Style"
is to a great extent synonymous with "Directory-Empire."
We are concerned with the Directory-Empire-Federal styles
of furniture only insofar as they show ornamentation.

AMERICAN EMPIRE CHAIR. Circa 1815.
Top slat, etched gold-leaf decoration; middle slat, carved out eagle,
gold-leafed and striped.   Fig.454

AMERICAN EMPIRE CHAIR. Circa 1815-1820. Finely executed
gold-leaf design on rosewood graining. Center slat stenciled in the manner of piano stenciling.   Fig.455

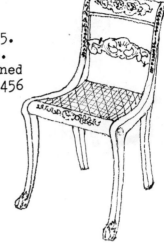

AMERICAN EMPIRE CHAIR. Circa 1815.
Possibly from Duncan Phyfe's shop.
Fine gold-leaf decoration on stained
wood.   Fig.456

AMERICAN EMPIRE CHAIR. Transitional
type. 1805-1825. Top rail painted
with a classic design. Larger than
usual. Curves around, with small
wooden knobs top and bottom. Fig.457

AMERICAN EMPIRE CHAIR. Transitional
type. Circa 1825-1835. Crosspiece
with anthemion. Gold-leaf decoration
on top rail, front of seat, and
stretcher. Rush seat. Crown-top
railing, seat front rolled. Probably
influenced Hitchcock and other later
styles.   Fig.458

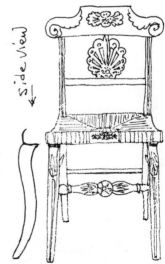

EMPIRE-SHERATON CHAIR. Transitional.
1815-1825. New York, New Jersey, and
Pennsylvania. Cut-out back, rolled-
over slat top. Black background with
gold leaf, burnt umber and red design.
Fig.459

EMPIRE-SHERATON CHAIR. Transitional. 1815-1825. New
York, New Jersey, and Pennsylvania. Stenciled.   Fig.460

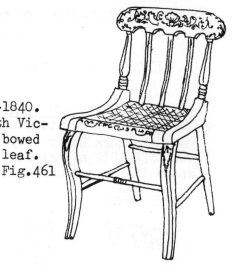

AMERICAN EMPIRE CHAIR. 1830-1840.
Late, transitional chair, with Victorian top rail. Cane seat, bowed
front legs. Design in metal leaf.
Fig.461

THE HITCHCOCK CHAIR

The Hitchcock chair is a derivation of the Sheraton fancy
chair and bears the name of the man who made it famous --
Lambert Hitchcock (1795-1852).

Most of Lambert Hitchcock's chairs were signed, from 1826
to 1832: "L.Hitchcock" and "Hitchcocks-ville. Conn. Warranted," and from 1832 to 1849, after going into business with
his brother-in-law: "Hitchcock. Alford. & Co Hitchcocks-
ville. Conn. Warranted." On the latter signature, the
"n's" were reversed.

There are undoubtedly many chairs made by Hitchcock which
were not signed, perhaps the most beautiful ones, on which
gold leaf as well as stenciling in bronze powders was used
as ornamentation. These may have been chairs made to in-
dividual order. The thousands that were shipped on consignment were evidently the ones that were signed.

The chair was widely imitated by his competitors. We refer to the signed chairs only as Hitchcock chairs, to the
others as "Hitchcock-style" chairs. For biographical notes
see HITCHCOCK under "Manufacturers and Manufactories."

HITCHCOCK.ALFORD.& Co HITCHCOCKS-VILLE. CONN.
WARRANTED.

L.HITCHCOCK.HITCHCOCKS-VILLE.CONN. WARRANTED.

HITCHCOCK CHAIR SIGNATURES. In the restored Hitchcock Chair Factory in Riverton, Connecticut, owned today by The Hitchcock Chair Co., the chairs and furniture bear the 1826-1832 signature with an encircled "R" added after the word "warranted." Fig.462 & 463

HITCHCOCK CHAIR. Button-back, crown-top. Connecticut. Circa 1835. Stenciled on a rosewood background. Cane seat. Signed "Hitchcock, Alford & Co., Hitchcocks-ville, Conn. - Warranted." Fig.464

HITCHCOCK STYLE CORNUCOPIA CHAIR. Slat back, bolster top. Connecticutt. Circa 1830. Rush seat. Stenciled fruit and leaves in the gold-leaf cornucopias. Gold turnings on the legs. Fig.465

HITCHCOCK CROWN-BACK & CROWN-TOP CHAIR. Connecticut. Circa 1830. Rush seat. Stenciled with two bronzes and signed "L. Hitchcock, Hitchcocksville Conn. - Warranted." Fig.466

HITCHCOCK-STYLE CUT-OUT SLAT CHAIR.
Pillow-top. America. Circa 1820.
Design mostly in gold leaf. Cane
seat.   Fig.467

HITCHCOCK-STYLE CUT-OUT SLAT CHAIR.
America. Circa 1824. Rush seat.
Gold-leaf design; found usually on a
black background.   Fig.468

HITCHCOCK-STYLE CHAIR. Diamond-shaped
slat-back with a pillow top. Connecticut. Circa 1832. Stenciled. Gold-
leaf turnings and yellow striping.
                              Fig.469

HITCHCOCK-STYLE EAGLE-BACK CHAIR.
Pillow top. Connecticut. Circa
1830. Rush seat, rare splayed legs
with many turnings. Gold-leaf eagle
and stenciling.   Fig.470

HITCHCOCK-STYLE EAGLE-BACK CHAIR.
Bolster top. Connecticut. Circa
1840. Plank seat, stenciled slat
and gilt turnings.   Fig.471

HITCHCOCK-STYLE ARMCHAIR. Narrow
slat-back. Connecticut. Circa 1830.
Rush seat, turned legs and a stenciled design.   Fig.472

HITCHCOCK-STYLE SLAT-BACK CHAIR.
Pillow top. America. Circa 1830.
Rush seat. Usually black, often
grained and stenciled.   Fig.473

HITCHCOCK-STYLE SLAT-BACK CHAIR.
Pillow top. Connecticut. 1825-
1839. Rush seat and bronze stenciling.   Fig.474

HITCHCOCK-STYLE SLAT-BACK CHAIR.
Roll-top rail. American. Circa
1845. Rush seat, black, grained.
Gold-leaf design.   Fig.475

HITCHCOCK-STYLE SLAT-BACK CHAIR.
Bolster top. Connecticut. Circa
1824. Rush seat. A narrow bar below the slat. Heavily grained background. Signed "William Moore, Jr."
on the back of the seat. He was a
storekeeper and chairmaker at "The
Fork of the River," which became
Hitchcocks-ville after 1835. Fig.476

HITCHCOCK-STYLE SLAT-BACK CHAIR.
Pillow top. New Hampshire. Circa
1840-1860. Plain leg style, grained
plank seat. The slat is stenciled
with basket and fruit, and the pillow
with pineapple and leaves. Signed
"J. K. Hatch, Warranted" under the
seat.   Fig.477

HITCHCOCK-STYLE SLAT-BACK CHAIR.
Slat top. Connecticut. 1839. Dark
green chair. The two slats and side
posts are stenciled in two-color
bronze over black. Plank seat.
Three spindles and different legs.
                              Fig.478

<u>HITCHCOCK</u> WINDSOR-TYPE CHAIR. Signed "Hitchcock, Alford
& C₀. Hitchcocks-ville, Conn. Warranted" (See Fig.463).
Circa 1832. Black chair with a bronze stencil used frequently on Hitchcock chairs. Plank seat. This chair is
interesting proof that the original Hitchcock factory also
made Windsor-type chairs.   Fig.479

HITCHCOCK-STYLE SLAT-BACK CHAIR.
Pillow top. America. Circa 1840.
Black, heavily grained. Stenciled,
striped, with a plank seat. Fig.480

HITCHCOCK-STYLE TURTLEBACK CHAIR.
Unusual crown-top shape. New York.
Circa 1827. Dark green, with the
turtle slat black. Stenciling
thought to be done by Gildersleeve
(1805-1871).   Fig.481

HITCHCOCK-STYLE TURTLEBACK CHAIR.
Pillow top. New York. Circa 1825.
Rush seat. Grained background with
stenciling on pillow top, slat, and
front roll. Possibly done by Ransom
Cook.   Fig.482

PENNSYLVANIA CHAIR. Cut-out slat.
1830-1840. Heavy brown and red graining with the design in yellow, olive,
and black. Pillow top is slightly
bowed and has a painted bird on it.
The narrow slat between the front
legs is also decorated.   Fig.483

PENNSYLVANIA CHAIR. "Angel-wing" top
slat. After 1825. Ends of the slats
are ornamented with metal leaf, polychrome painting and freehand bronze.
Plank seat.   Fig.484

PENNSYLVANIA CHAIR. Balloon back.
1850. Stenciled design with transparent washes on a dark brown background.
This type of chair also came in green
and black.   Fig.485

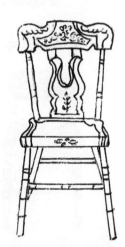

PENNSYLVANIA CHAIR. Boot-jack splat
back. Angel wing rail. Lancaster
County. 1850. Executed in a crude,
bold manner, in bright clear colors.
Background is Dutch pink.   Fig.486

PENNSYLVANIA CHAIR. Slat-back, slat-
top. Circa 1825. Background medium
green. Scenic panels are framed with
broad stripes of transparent brown
and black. Gold leaf trimming. Well
striped.   Fig.487

ROCKING CHAIRS

BALLOON BACK ROCKING CHAIR. Pennsylvania. Circa 1825. The design is
stenciled, with transparent washes.
Dark background.   Fig.488

BOSTON ROCKER. 1820-1840.   Fig.489

The Boston rocker has a wooden seat that curves up at the
rear and is rolled at the front. The sides are slightly
cyma-curved. The legs are short, turned at front, plain
at rear, and are mounted on short rockers. The high back
usually has 7 to 9 spindles. The top rail is wide, arched, and has rounded ends.

The early Boston rocker has one thing in common with the
Hitchcock-style chair, and that is its stenciled ornamentation. On the late Victorian rockers, the design is frequently stenciled and painted.

This type rocking chair probably originated in Boston,
but they were made elsewhere, too. Here we have an
analogy with the "Philadelphia" highboy, which was made
also in other furniture centers.

To all appearances, the Boston rocker developed from the
Windsor rocking chair, which rarely showed any decoration.

Some -- the later ones -- are quite clumsy, but they are
comfortable, and give a traditional touch to a room. They
were made in standardized form from 1840 to as late as 1890.
Today we are enjoying a revival of the Boston rocker, as of
all old Americana.

BOSTON ROCKER. Connecticut. Circa
1832. Typical Hitchcock stenciling
and pattern. Grained, black chair.
                              Fig.490

BOSTON ROCKER. Boston. Circa 1840.
Slat top is stenciled, all cut in
one piece: birds, nest, and fruit.
                              Fig.491

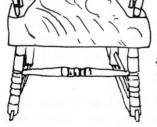

BOSTON ROCKER. Circa 1845. Has
heavy rolled and grained seat and a
lower back than most Boston rockers.
Light, straight spindles and a heavy
top rail.   Fig.492

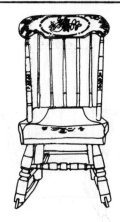

CHILD'S ROCKING CHAIR. Boston rocker
style. West Winsted, Connecticut.
Made by the Union Chair Company.
Strawberry stencil with bronzed scrolls
on the top slat. Front seat roll
stenciled.   Fig.493

CHILD'S ROCKING CHAIR. Pennsylvania
German. 1840-1850. 25 1/4" high x
14 1/2". Square seat. Cream background. Design: leaves and stylized
units in bronze. Many stripes.
                              Fig.494

COMB-BACK ROCKING CHAIR. Windsor
style. Early 1800's. Dark brown
background, white flowers with vermilion accents. The front of the
seat and the rungs are decorated, as
are the rockers and two top slats.
                              Fig.495

HITCHCOCK ROCKING CHAIR. With Salem-
style seat. Signed "Hitchcock & Alford, Hitchcocks-ville, Conn." Circa
1830. Stenciled design on side posts,
legs, and chair back.   Fig.496

HITCHCOCK ROCKING CHAIR. 1826-1832.
Signed L. Hitchcock piece with a
very high back. Pillow top. Three
bow spindles and rush seat. The
back, pillow, and front of seat are
stenciled.   Fig.497

Fig.498

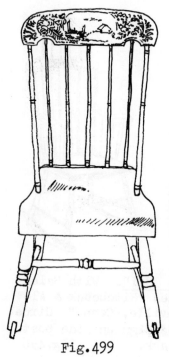

LADY ROCKERS. Also called "mammy,"
"nursing," and "grandma" rockers.
Boston rocker style, with no arms.
Circa 1840-1850. 34" tall; 16 1/2"
by 16 1/2" seat (Fig.498). On this
rocker the top slat is stenciled,
the front roll also. In the other
chair (Fig.499) only the top slat is
stenciled in the William Eaton style,
a scene framed with scroll work.
                            Fig.498 & 499

Fig.499

THE SALEM-TYPE ROCKING CHAIR

In contrast to the Boston rocker, the Salem rocker has a
seat rounded at the back, and a Windsor-type seat front,
not rolled. Frequently found in yellow.

SALEM-TYPE ROCKING CHAIR. With Boston rocker and Windsor features.
Windsor-type seat. Step-down rail,
stenciled. Yellow background. Bowed
spindles. Also called a "Windsor"
rocker.   Fig.500

SALEM-TYPE ROCKING CHAIR. Circa
1830. Yellow background, natural
arms. Stenciled and painted design. Bowed spindles.   Fig.501

ROCKER SETTEES

These probably were first made by a New England house-
holder for his wife and child, the wife on the seat, the
baby in the cradle section. From 1760.

SETTEE or CRADLE ROCKER. New England. 1785-1840. Stenciled, painted, and beautifully striped on a rosewood-
grained black background. Sometimes called a "Cape Cod"
or "mammy" rocker.   Fig.502

SHERATON & SHERATON FANCY CHAIRS

SHERATON ARMCHAIR.   England. Circa
1780. Mahogany painted background
with a simple painted design of leaves
and bows. Cane seat and tapered legs.
                                  Fig.503

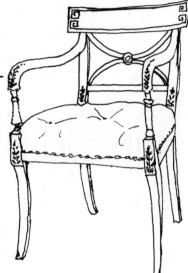

SHERATON ARMCHAIR. England. Circa 1815. A late Sheraton chair with broad crested rail over the side uprights. S-shaped arms and splayed legs. Stained wood and gold-leaf decoration.   Fig.504

SHERATON FANCY CHAIR. America. 1800-1826. Octagonal panel in the open-slat back; slat top. Rush seat. Stenciling and Greek scrolling. Greek key design on apron.   Fig.505

SHERATON FANCY CHAIR. America. 1800-1826. Bowed front stretcher, splayed legs and a rush seat. Black background with gilt and bronze design. Stripes on the narrow apron. Three bars and two bars with gilt balls make up the "fancy" back.   Fig.506

SHERATON ARMCHAIR. America. Circa 1826. Rush seat. Stenciling on a grained background. Also called a "fancy" chair.   Fig.507

SHERATON FANCY ARMCHAIR. New York. 1810-1920. Off-white background with design of shells, tassels, and drapery in shaded gold leaf. Striped arm braces and lattice slat back
                                                                    Fig.508

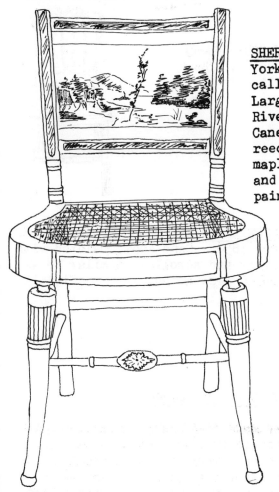

SHERATON FANCY CHAIR. New
York. Circa 1917. A so-
called "landscape" chair.
Large slat with a Hudson
River scene painted on it.
Cane seat. Splayed and
reeded frint legs. Curly
maple graining. Stripes
and bands in red-brown
paint and gold leaf.
Fig.509

VICTORIAN CHAIRS

VICTORIAN CHAIR. American Empire,
transitional. Circa 1850. Rows of
leaves in gilt on the stiles and
legs. Painted scrolls on slats,
cane seat, and splayed legs. Fig.510

VICTORIAN CHAIR. American. Circa
1850. A very popular chair. Cane
seat and stenciled fruit with color
washes.   Fig.511

VICTORIAN CHAIR, CHILD'S. American.
Circa 1850. Cane seat, painted with
flowers and scrolls. Similar to Wm.
Eaton's decoration.   Fig.512

WINDSOR-STYLE CHAIRS

American Windsor Chairs were first made in Philadelphia,
circa 1725. They became so popular that they were soon
made in the other colonies. They were of several different kinds of wood, for structural purposes, and were
painted. In early days the most common color was deep
green.

There is little room for decoration on the early Windsors
but sometimes one finds a small freehand painted design
on the top slat and some painted "rings" and striping.
The American Windsors have raked legs and spindle backs,
whereas the typical English Windsors have straight legs
and a center splat. Those which are of interest to us
in this glossary are the 19th century descendents of the
early Windsor because of their freehand and stenciled decoration.

WINDSOR-STYLE ARROWBACK CHAIR. American. Circa 1820-1835. Comes with
3, 4, or 5 arrow-shaped spindles.
These chairs were painted yellow,
cream, green, red, and mottled, with
a colorful painted design on the top
slat and arrows. Windsor descent.
                                Fig.513

WINDSOR-STYLE CHAMBER or INVALID
CHAIR. New York. Circa 1850-1860.
Stenciled and striped on black.
The lower part of the top slat is
scalloped. Possibly a Robinson
piece.   Fig.514

WINDSOR-STYLE FANBACK CHAIR. Pennsylvania. Circa 1800. Saddle seat,
brush stroke painting on a light
background.   Fig.515

WINDSOR-STYLE HIGH CHAIR. New England, 1860. Rosewood grained chair
with a one-piece stencil. Design:
rose and leaves.   Fig.516

WINDSOR-STYLE PENNSYLVANIA CHAIR.
From 1725. Stick construction of
rail, arms, and side posts is square
instead of the typical round. Dark
brown striping and brush strokes on
a "greenish putty" base coat. Bamboo legs and H stretcher are decorated the same as above. The saddle
seat is dark green.   Fig.517

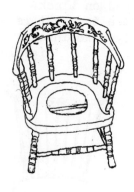

WINDSOR-STYLE POTTY CHAIR. American.
Circa 1860. 24" tall. Seat 14" x
14". Design light brown scrolls and
odd stylized flowers painted with
vermilion accents on a dark brown
background.   Fig.518

WINDSOR-STYLE THUMBBACK CHAIR. American, 1830-1845. A Windsor descent,
yellow background, stenciled and freehand painted plank seat, striped,
with a narrow black stripe and a wide
brown one. Sometimes called a "rab-
bit ear" chair, or a "common yellow"
chair, but not a "thumbnail" chair.
                               Fig.519

WINDSOR-STYLE JOHN WHITE CHAIR. With
yoke slat back. Vermont. Circa
1838. John White's chairs were handmade, therefore varied slightly.
With their plank seats they were useful in many ways, and sturdy. Legs
and rungs of this one are bamboo-type.
Base coat, red brown; design, cream
with green sprays. The legs are
striped white all the way round. His
chairs were made in Woodstock, Vermont. See JOHN WHITE under "Painters
and Craftsman."   Fig.520

WINDSOR-STYLE WILDER CHAIR. Step-
down slat-back. New Ipswich, New
Hampshire. 1810-1835. Design: gold
leaf shell with "sweeping" grasses
and brush strokes.   Fig.521

WINDSOR-STYLE YOUTH CHAIR, or HIGH
CHAIR. American. 1850-1870. 34"
tall, 12 1/2" seat. On a black,
lightly grained base coat, it has
white striping and flower painting.
                                Fig.522

CHESTS

GILLAM CHESTS,   see   SAYBROOK CHESTS

GUILFORD CHESTS,   see   SAYBROOK CHESTS

MASSACHUSETTS CHEST. Circa 1850. Painted with a typical design of homesteads and farms. The stained top is one color; the rest is another. Simple painting.   Fig.523

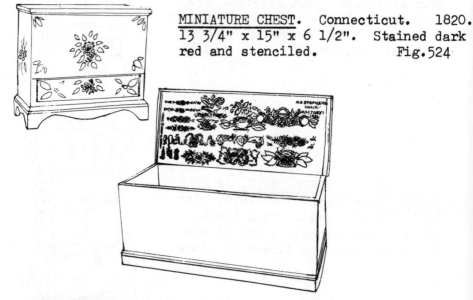

MINIATURE CHEST. Connecticut.   1820. 13 3/4" x 15" x 6 1/2".   Stained dark red and stenciled.   Fig.524

NEW YORK CHEST. 1832   The top is stenciled inside with chair designs. Labelled: "N. R. Stephens Chair Factory." Probably a salesman's chest.   Fig.525

Of the PENNSYLVANIA CHEST it may be said, roughly, that
Berks County was renowned for the unicorn in its designs.
Dauphin County went in frequently for floral motifs.
Montgomery and Lehigh preferred the geometrical design.
Sunken arched panels and columns and the tulip were favored by Lebanon County. In Lancaster County, chests
were often painted a mottled green with white panels on
top and arched panels in front. However, Christian Seltzer, of Lebanon County, gave us a beautiful red-brown
chest with white panels and flowers, always with brown
leaves, springing from large pewter tankards.

The counties in all probability had no set design, and
so many were brought over from "the old country" it may
be safest to say that chests, designed as just described,
were most frequently found in these respective counties.

PENNSYLVANIA DOWRY CHEST. Berks County. 1797. 4' 6"
long. Two arched panels, decorated, in front, and two
panels on top. All have white backgrounds. Unicorns,
symbolizing maidenly virtue, make up the center design.
Two drawers at bottom. Bracket feet. A signed and
dated piece.   Fig.526

PENNSYLVANIA DOWRY CHEST. Montgomery County. 1780-1800.
About 22" high, 40" long. Trifoliate-shaped panels
done with geometric accuracy. The decoration is severe-
ly stylized tulips, with parrots or doves used occasionally, but it is mainly floral. Thistles and persimmons
are also used.   Fig.527

PENNSYLVANIA DOWRY CHEST. Lancaster County. 1787.
Sponge graining on a blue background. White panels with
tulip designs. The panels are typically sunken. Upper
front sponge painted.   Fig.528

PENNSYLVANIA DOWRY CHEST. Lancaster County. Circa 1788.
Birds or unicorns form the major parts of the design.
Sometimes parrots, doves, or pheasants are used. Tulips
and carnations are grouped around the focal points. This
chest is gayly decorated. Three sunken panels on the
front. The center one is pointed and the two flanking
panels are elliptical in shape. All are painted. The
upper section is grained.   Fig.529

PENNSYLVANIA DOWRY CHEST. Lebanon County. Painted by
Christian Seltzer, dated 1784. 4'2" long. Red-brown
background. Two white front panels painted. Two large
tankards with colorful tulips, brown leaves framed by a
border of flowers. Seltzer painted this type of chest
until 1792.   Fig.530

PENNSYLVANIA DOWRY CHEST. Lebanon County. Painted by
John Seltzer, 1805, son of Christian. Approximately
4' 3" long. Deeply stained chest with three front panels,
white, on which are painted polychrome flowers and rare
birds issuing forth from narrow vases and a wine glass.
                                                      Fig.531

PENNSYLVANIA DOWRY CHEST. Lebanon County. Circa 1721.
The panels are not clearly defined but are divided by
posts resembling turned balusters and human figures
which may be the bride and groom. The front decoration,
in heavy coloring, consists of vases of branching tulips
and 4-, 5-, or 6-petaled flowers.   Fig.532

PENNSYLVANIA DOWRY CHEST. Lebanon County. Circa 1730.
Simulated architectural arches and columns. Design:
polychromed flowers and a stippled or putty-grained
background, surrounding the arches.   Fig.533

PENNSYLVANIA CHEST. Lehigh County, 1805. Varied panel
shapes and a large one on the top. Six-petaled star on
the sides. Floral decoration, and grained background.
The bride's name and date are painted on the chest.
                                                     Fig.534

SAYBROOK (OR GILLAM) CHESTS

Formerly called Guilford chests, a designation put very
much in doubt by an article in the Connecticut Historical
Society Bulletin, Volume 23, No.1, January 1958, by William W. Warren, entitled "Were the Guilford-Painted
Chests made in Saybrook?"

SAYBROOK CHEST. Connecticut. Circa 1700. With drawers.
A design of meandering vines, birds, and flowers on a
stained red background. Possibly done by Charles Gillam.

Fig.535

SAYBROOK CHEST. Connecticut. Circa 1700. Now thought
to be decorated by Charles Gillam. Painted a purplish
brown, with white, green, and red scrolls and flower
decorations on the front, and a painted goose at each
end.   Fig.536

SEA CHEST. Might be from Massachusetts. Circa 1750.
46" x 18 1/2" x 26". The painting depicts a story from
which we can date the piece. A six-dowelled chest.
                                                       Fig.537

TAUNTON BLANKET CHEST. Taunton, Massachusetts.   1724-
1740. Robert Crossman, furniture and drum maker, produced the vine tree-of-life design in white on brown or
natural wood. At a later point he added birds and
tulips.   Fig.538

TAUNTON BLANKET CHEST, with drawers. Taunton, Massachusetts. 1730.   21" long x 20 1/2" high x 12 1/2" wide.
By Robert Crossman. Design: a spray of painted leaves
on the front and two on the drawer.   Fig.539

CHEST OF DRAWERS, or BUREAU.
Connecticut. Circa 1820.
Stenciled in Hitchcock style.
Scroll supports hold the rectangular mirror; they are also
stenciled. The top has three
small drawers and under this a
cushion frieze concealing a
drawer, stenciled with fruit
and flowers, with two rosettes.
At the ends of three recessed
drawers are columns with acanthus leaf stencils. The piece
stands on turned feet and is
purported to have been made by
Lambert Hitchcock.   Fig.540

CHEST-ON-CHEST
(Highboy)

HIGHBOY. Also called "chest-on-
chest" or "chest-of-drawers."
Boston. Circa 1700. Wood,
japanned in black, with gold-
leaf chinoiserie design in relief. Also known as a flat top
highboy. 5' 3 1/2" tall.
                      Fig.541

LOW CHEST, or LOW BOY. Possibly Boston. Circa 1700.
Design: gold-leaf chinoiserie pattern in relief, cabriole
legs.   Fig.542

CRADLES

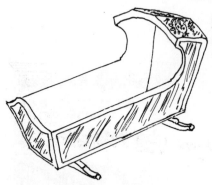

CRADLE. American. Circa 1840.
Approximately 33" x 18" x 22".
Background: red graining over
black. The hood is stenciled.
Inside: buttermilk red.Fig.543

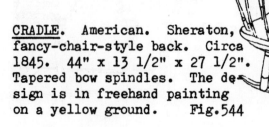

CRADLE. American. Sheraton,
fancy-chair-style back. Circa
1845. 44" x 13 1/2" x 27 1/2".
Tapered bow spindles. The design is in freehand painting
on a yellow ground.   Fig.544

KAST. Frequently called "kas." A cupboard or wardrobe, Dutch in origin. 18th century. Often paneled and painted, rarely carved, with two doors, heavy cornices and usually one or two drawers at the bottom. These three examples are painted in grisailles, or grey monochrome, which makes the work look three dimensional.

KAST. Approximately 74 1/2" high, 58" wide, and 19 3/4" deep. Circa 1690. Found in Saugerties, New York. Fig. 545

KAST. 7' tall, 75" wide, and 24 3/4" deep. Two drawers at the bottom.
Fig. 546

KAST. A rare example of a Hudson Valley kast, 1700.
Approximately 88" high, 75" wide and 24 3/4" deep. A
fine example of <u>trompe l'oeil</u> painting in <u>grisaille</u>.
Fig.547

MINIATURE FURNITURE

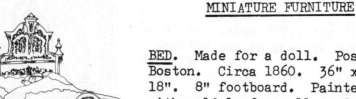

BED. Made for a doll. Possibly
Boston. Circa 1860. 36" x 20" x
18". 8" footboard. Painted black,
with gold-leaf scrolls and opaque
flower painting. Could have been
painted by Thomas Hill of Gardner,
Massachusetts.   Fig.548

CHAIR. Circa 1860. Made by the
Heywood, Wakefield Company in Gardner, Massachusetts. Attributed to
Thomas Hill, an employee. Approximately 10" tall; black, grained
background. Decorated with pink
roses and gold scrolls.   Fig.549

PIANO

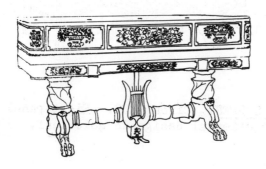

PIANO. New York. Circa 1820. Combined stenciling and
freehand bronze stump work gives us the name "piano stenciling". Lovely early work. Baskets in gold leaf, model-
ed leaves, composite flowers and rounded plums on mahogany
grained background.   Fig.550

SCREEN

COROMANDEL SCREEN. Circa 1800. Eight-panel. Brown background with oriental design in gold leaf. 10'6" x 83"
high.   Fig.551

SECRETARIES

SECRETARY BOOKCASE. Massachusetts. Circa 1800. Oval
looking glasses bordered by églomisé panels. Vases,
bouquets, and scenes of ladies picking and arranging
flowers make up the design. Mahogany case. Figured
veneer on drawers and doors.   Fig.552

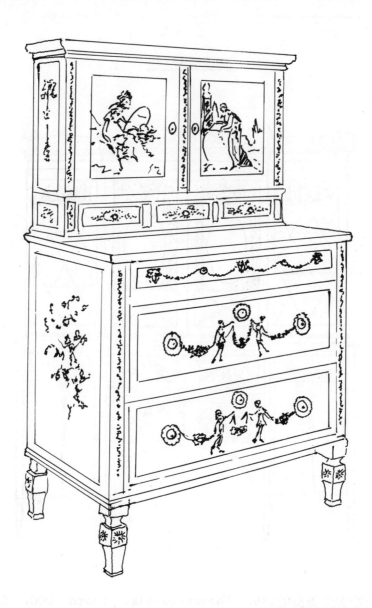

SECRETARY, GERMAN. By F. G. Weitsch (1758-1828). Signed
and dated 1794. Decorated with allegorical painting,
japanned on tin. Polychromed. Brass details on legs and
drawers.   Fig.553

SETTEES

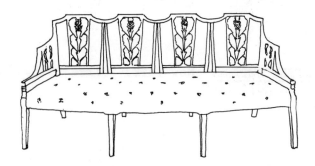

<u>ADAM-HEPPLEWHITE SETTEE</u>. England. 1800-1810. 38 1/2"
tall, 64" long, painted on the four splats and arms.
Also called a four-chair-back settee. See note attached
to Fig.443.   Fig.554

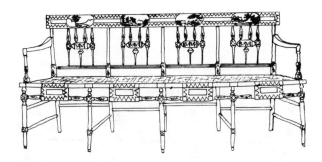

<u>BALTIMORE SETTEE</u>. With strong Sheraton influence. A
typical Baltimore piece. Circa 1810-1815. 38 1/2" tall
by 68" long. Signed "Thos. Renshaw, No. 37 S. Gay St.,
Balti- John Barnhart, Ornamenter." Four scenes of local
landscapes on the back rail. A decorative and structural
design carried through the slats, balusters, and legs.
                                                   Fig.555

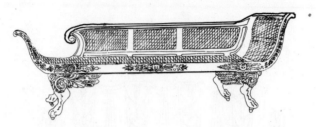

GRECIAN STYLE SETTEE. New York. Circa 1815. Caned and
decorated in gold leaf.   Fig.556

Detail of Fig.556

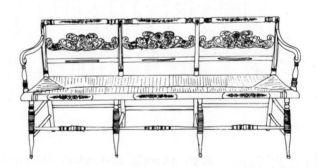

HITCHCOCK-STYLE SETTEE. Connecticut. Circa 1830. 33"
tall, 57" long, 18" deep. Turned legs and a rush seat.
The cornucopias, roll tops, and front seat rolls are
stenciled.   Fig.557

NEW YORK SETTEE and FOLDING BED. Early 19th century.
Undoubtedly painted by a trained English artist. Design freehand bronze fruit and leaves on a white background.   Fig.558

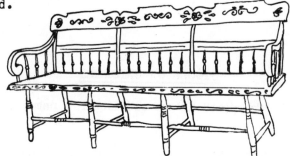

PENNSYLVANIA SETTEE or BENCH. 1850. 7' long, 22" wide.
Gaily painted top rail in Pennsylvania German motifs.
Bar crosspiece with 18 spindles. Many colored back-
grounds were used.   Fig.559

WINDSOR-STYLE SETTEE. With step-down slat. American.
1827. 7' long, 21 1/2" wide. The top rail is decorated with a brush-stroke painting. Probably a John
White bench.   Fig.560

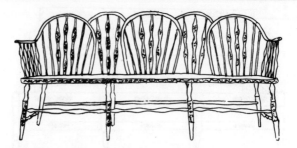

WINDSOR-STYLE SETTEE. Philadelphia. 1800. 7' x 21 1/4"
wide. A painted running leaf pattern on the balusters
and along the front of seat.   Fig.561

STOOLS OR CRICKETS

"Cricket" is an old English name

STOOL. New England. Mid-1800's. Boldly grained in
red and black. Design: pink flower surrounded by green
brush-stroke leaves, and bordered by a wide green band;
stripe and tendrils, yellow. 7 1/2" wide x 11 7/8" long
x 6 1/2" high.   Fig.562

STOOL. New England. 19th century. 12 1/4" long x 8"
wide x 10" high. Stenciled on a grained background.
Fig.563

TABLES

CARD TABLE. Baltimore. 1800-1810. Made by Robert
Fisher. Japanned with gold-leaf and painted design.
Musical instruments are painted on the octagon side
panels. Painted lines down the legs resemble reeding.
Note the similarity to the Baltimore chair and settee,
Fig.445 and 555.   Fig.564

<u>DINING TABLE</u>. New York. Circa 1830. A stenciled mahogany table, in style according to the last phase of the so-called classical type.   Fig.565

<u>DROP-LEAF TABLE</u>. England. 18th century, with so-called "Indian" decoration. Japanned in black.
          Fig.566

<u>DROP-LEAF TABLE</u>. New England. Circa 1840. Lambert Hitchcock made tables like this a little earlier. This one has a simple stenciled border on a mahogany grained background.
          Fig.567

PEDESTAL TABLE or CANDLE STAND. England. Circa 1750. Also called a
"torchère." Design:gold leaf on
black background.   Fig.569

END TABLE. Connecticut. 1830-1840.
Stenciled design, with yellow and
green banding on the legs. Grained
background. 28 1/4" high x 18 1/2"
wide x 15 3/4" deep.   Fig.568

PEDESTAL TABLE. New Hampshire. Circa 1830. Detail of
the top shown in center. The decanter and tumbler shown
at the right, both made of wood, were made by the same
craftsman. This is miscalled a "Persian" table. Part
of the design is block printed. The background is a rich
copper bronze. The top has an ornamented circle with a
stylized Persian bird, edged with curving scrolls and
red and black leaves. Rosettes are block printed outside
the design, probably a labor-saving device.   Fig.570

PEMBROKE TABLE. Also called a "breakfast" table. England. Circa 1790. 40 3/4" long x 22 1/4" wide x 28 1/4" high. Gilded carving on the legs. Sheraton style of tapering and rounding of legs. Drawer with two brass pulls on end. Painted flower garlands. Rarely found with painted decoration. Not unlike Angelica Kauffmann's work. Fig.571

TILT-TOP or TIP-UP TABLE. England. Circa 1770. 28 3/4" x 20" x 29". Gold-leaf design on the tripod pedestal base. Pontypool rectangular metal tray, japanned, serves as the top. Lace-edge painting of fruits and flowers in the well. The scalloped or lobed sides of the well are bordered below by a blue-grey band edged with gold leaf. The straight edges of the flat rim are bordered by a pierced edge and spandrels, which have embossed painting in gold leaf. Fig.573

TILT-TOP or TIP-UP TABLE. Scalloped edge, japanned in
black. Circa 1750. Chinese influence in the oriential
decoration. English. Possible Birmingham. Lacquered
wood, not papier-mâché.   Fig.572

WASHSTANDS

WASHSTAND, with splashboard. Connecticut. 1826-1843. Design stenciled on a dark grained background. Lambert Hitchcock is known to have made many variations of similar washstands.
Fig.574

WASHSTAND, with splashboard. New England. Mid-19th century. Design: freehand bronze on an off-white background.   Fig.575

WASHSTAND, with splashboard. New England. Late 19th century. Background yellow, with brown striping, the design is executed in freehand bronze and stenciling over a black pattern, with freehand work. A fine example of putty graining on lower platform.   Fig.576

SYMBOLS

Traditional ornamentation abounds with forms and details
that originally were invested with a meaning that was dis-
regarded as the design gradually came to be used solely
for decorative purposes.

Traditionally these motifs may have been symbolic of vic-
tory, defeat, sacrifice, and all manner of religious sig-
nificance.

 <u>ACORN</u>. Welcome.   Fig.577

<u>ANGEL</u>. Pennsylvania motif. Goodness, purity.   Fig.578

<u>BARN SIGNS</u>. Pennsylvania German. Considered to have a
purely decorative purpose. In the 20th century called
"hex signs." "Hex," in German, means "witch." Whether
the signs were intended to ward off evil spirits remains
controversial.   Fig.579

CORNUCOPIA. Horn of plenty, overflow-
ing with fruit, flowers, etc.Fig.580

HEART. Pennsylvania motif. Love.
                                    Fig.581

IVY. Life eternal, because of its
eternal green; fidelity because of
the way it clings to its support.
                                    Fig.582

LILY. Purity.   Fig.583

LILIES OF PEACE OR LOVE, growing on
the tree of life which is fed by God's
goodness and grace. Two leaves at
the bottom.   Fig.584

LINE OF LIFE, its ups and downs, be-
ginning and end.   Fig.585

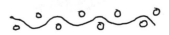

OAK LEAF. Faith and endurance.
                                    Fig.586

OLIVE BRANCH. Peace.   Fig.587

PEACOCK. Pennsylvania German. Resurrection.   Fig.588

PEACOCK, looking back at his tail.
Pennsylvania German. Rebirth.
                                 Fig.589

PEACOCK. The blue dot is "the eye of
God." Pennsylvania German. Fig.590

RED CARNATION. Pure love. Fig.591

CHERRY. Good works.   Fig.592

CHRISTMAS ROSE. The nativity.
                              Fig.593

DISTELFINK. Pennsylvania German.
Goldfinch.   Fig.594

DOVES. Pennsylvania German. Peace. Found frequently
on frakturs.   Fig.595

EAGLES

The eagle has been the emblem of conquerors for over three
thousand years. Rome, Austria, Prussia, and France under
the Empire adopted it as their royal emblem. In heraldry
it is considered a charge of honor. Yet it took six
years to decide that the American eagle was to become our
national symbol.

Between 1772 and 1779, an itinerant decorator painted an
eagle with olive branch and arrows on a wall in Washington, Connecticut. It bore the motto "Federal Union." At

the close of the revolution, the American eagle as a symbol of liberty had become an inspiration to the American
colonist. When George Washington made his triumphant
tour, transparent painted eagles, sketched on paper, were
placed against the window panes of houses along his route,
with lighted candles behind them. Craftsmen were eager
to depict the regal bird. Potters, sign makers, wood
carvers, glass makers, printers, weavers, button makers,
even the housewife displayed the eagle on her quilts,
rugs, and needlework. To all of them the new symbol sig-
nified virility, pride, and majesty.

England, eager to recapture a promising market, flooded
the Colonies with the new symbol of freedom. Eagles
could be found on clocks, fabrics, buttons, china, and
glass, in fact on almost any object on which the bird,
carved or painted, could be reasonably applied. In
Marblehead, Massachusetts, sea captains placed carved
eagles over their doors as a sign that a captain lived
within. Since these days, the eagle as a decorative unit
has held precedence over all others in these United
States.

AMERICAN BALD EAGLE. Symbolically the eagle's head turns
right except in the case of death or in memoriam. When
the head is turned right (dexter) it signifies peace; to
the left (sinister), war.   Fig.596

The eagle sinister, or facing left.   Fig.597

The eagle dexter, or facing right.   Fig.598

EAGLE FINIALS

EAGLE FINIAL, in a landing or taking off position. May be found on Simon Willard presentation timepieces.
Fig.599

EAGLE FINIAL. Used by Simon Willard apprentices.   Fig.600

SPREAD EAGLES. This type was never used by Simon Willard.
Fig.601

PHOENIX. In heraldry called a "demi-
eagle" and frequently mistaken for
an eagle. Fabled to live 500 years
and be capable of consuming itself
by fire only to rise in youthful
freshness out of its own ashes. Hence
a symbol of immortality, and in
Christian art, of resurrection.

Fig.602

PINE TREE. Good luck.   Fig.603

PINEAPPLE. Hospitality.   Fig.604

POMEGRANATE. Fertility, the hope of
immortality, and resurrection, because of the unity of many seeds in
one fruit. Also a religious motif.
Pennsylvania German.   Fig.605

ROSE. Secrecy.   Fig.606

STARS

STAR. Pennsylvania German.   Regener-
ation.   Fig.607

FIVE-POINTED STAR. Pennsylvania German. Personality.   Fig.608

EIGHT-POINTED STAR. Pennsylvania German. Spirit of perfection. Fig.609

STRAWBERRY. Righteousness, the fruit-
fulness of the spirit.   Fig.610

SUN. Pennsylvania German. Signifies
daytime.   Fig.611

THISTLE.   Earthly sorrow and sin.
                            Fig.612A

THISTLE.   Earthly sorrow and sin.
                            Fig.612B

TOMATO or LOVE APPLE. Pennsylvania
German motif.   Fig.613

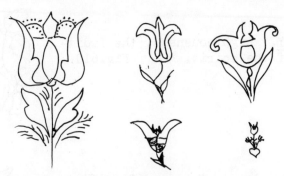

<u>TULIPS</u>. The most popular motif. May have originated in Turkey. Found frequently on chests. A Pennsylvania motif, but also found in other states.   Fig.614

<u>TRINITY TULIP</u>. Religious motif.
                                                    Fig.615

<u>UNICORN</u>. Signifies the protection of maidenly virtue. On chests and frakturs, mainly.   Fig.616

<u>WHEAT SPRAY</u>. Fidelity, also bounty. A religious motif.   Fig.617

DESIGNS

BARGEE ART, or "Roses and Castles," which adorned the
canal boats of England and Wales in the 18th, 19th, and
early 20th centuries. The castle stood for honor, the
heart for romance, the rose for beauty.

BARGEE ART, COFFEE POT. Circa 1840. Roses on borders,
scenic castle in center, painted in bright colors.
                                                      Fig.618

BARGEE ART, embellished cabin DOOR
PANEL. Circa 1803. 12" x 30". From
a lavishly decorated canal boat.
Stoke Bruerne. On the Grand Union
Canal.   Fig.619

BARGEE ART, WATER CAN. Circa 1861.
Tinplate painted dark blue, very gaily
decorated.   Fig.620

CRYSTALLIZED TIN, a method introduced by Mr. Vallet of
Wolverhampton, England in the early 1800s. Tin, acid-
washed to give it a pattern of high lights and frosted
spots. Over this was applied different colored washes
or asphaltum.

DALMALING OR VALLEY PAINTING

About 1780 a genre of ceiling or mural painting, referred
to as Dalmaling, arose around Lake Siljan in the Swedish
province of Dalarna. This ornamental folk-art was the
creation of craftsmen whose original occupation was the
painting of patterns on furniture, and who traveled in
prosperous parts of the country, selling their wares. A
decorative style developed in the ornamentation of cup-
boards and the like. A deeply rooted belief of the common people in Dalarna that their environment of timbered
homes was the Holy Land is expressed in "Dala" painting
in a unique form which lacks an equivalent in world folk
art. Leksand and Rattvik became the centers for this
style of painting which lasted for nearly a hundred years.
The colors of the Rattvik school were dominantly red and
green; Leksand used mainly blue, ochre, and red. The
paintings were always done on white backgrounds.

<u>DALMALING</u> or <u>VALLEY PAINTING</u>. Leksand, 1827. 41" x 50".
A New Testament scene: Jesus on the Mount of Tabor.
"Jesus taketh Peter, James, and John, and brings them up
into an high mountain apart. There appeared unto them
Moses and Elias talking with him. And a bright cloud
overshadowed them; and behold a voice out of the cloud,
which said: 'This is my beloved Son, hear ye him.'"

Fig.621

DALMALING WALL HANGING. Circa 1840, by Daniel Andersson.
26" x 40". From Rattvik, in the county of Dalarna, Sweden.
A New Testament scene.   Fig.622

GRAINING

Painting or staining to imitate the grain of wood, marble, etc. The wood used in chairs, bureaus, washstands, etc. was often grained to simulate more expensive woods, such as rosewood.

GRAINING ON ASPHALTUM BACKGROUND OF COUNTRY TIN

This form of graining has been attributed to Mercy North of Fly Creek, N.Y., since many pieces resembling her style of decoration seem to have this type of background. Some-times it appears in almost straight lines of black or a deeper tone of asphaltum, painted at intervals and run-ning vertically, horizontally, or slantwise throughout the lighter asphaltum background. At other times it runs in a zig-zag fashion or in separated elongated spots. We have no records that explain this technique which at times seems to have been painted under or into the asphaltum, at others applied by some tool, possibly a corncob, roll-ed across the surface.

FEATHER GRAINING

The article was first painted flat black or other colors. When dry it was grained with a turkey feather, trimmed one inch wide. The feather was dipped in a thin mixture of contrasting paint and drawn on its side across the pan-el and down the stiles (of a chair). Also found on frames, chests, etc.

MARBLING

A smoked effect which resembled marble was produced by varnishing over a dry surface and, when tacky, passing a lighted candle near the surface, quickly enough for the smoke to adhere to the varnish, but not to blacken or

blister it.   This was usually done over a yellow or white
painted background.

Another kind of marbling was found on floors, woodwork,
chests, etc.   After the background color had been allowed
to dry thoroughly, the surface was coated with a thin
glaze of color, either contrasting or a deeper shade of
the same color, black, or white, depending on the desired
effect.   While still wet, spots were wiped out at irre-
gular intervals with brush, feather, etc., the results
reflecting the skill of the craftsman.

PUTTY GRAINING

This type was usually found on yellow painted wooden seats
and chests.   When the yellow background paint was dry, a
thin coat of a mixture of dry umber pigment and vinegar
was applied.   While wet, putty was used to "pounce out"
a design.   Rolled in a long thin roll, it could be held
in place at one end while the grainer pounced the other
in a semi-circle to form interesting shell and seaweed
patterns.

ROSEWOOD GRAINING

To imitate rosewood, the piece was first painted a dull
red and allowed to dry.   A thin coat of flat black paint
was then applied and quickly removed in streaks to imitate the grain of wood.   For this purpose crumpled newspaper, heavy netting, etc. were used.   A second method
was to apply the flat black paint with a pinked brush
which painted the graining over the red undercoat.   The
old-timers also painted on the flat black, removing some
of it by means of metal combs in various sizes to form
the graining pattern.

STIPPLING

Sometimes called "mottling" or "sponging." On a dry
background a coarse sponge dipped into paint was touched
evenly over a surface to produce interesting effects. A
corncob was used to achieve a different effect.

GRAINING ON TIN

In the early 1860's imitation wood graining appeared on
metal trays in the English market. Walnut graining was
the most popular and the most successfully imitated.

WALNUT GRAINING

The methods listed under rosewood graining were applied
to walnut graining, the difference being that the thin
black paint was used directly over maple or pine. It was
used on metal trays in the 1860's.

KROTING. Ceiling decoration done in chalk. Ramberg,
Heddal, Telemark, painted by Olav Hansson, 1781. White
background, acanthus tendrils, flowers in blue, red, and
yellow, the beams in pink and brown. Norway.   Fig.623

DESIGN ON MATERIALS

COVERLET. Connecticut, early 19th century. Detail, sten-
ciled in green, yellow, and orange on unbleached cotton.
Note how the bottom corners were cut out. Signed Hannah
Corbin.   Fig.624

FLOOR CLOTH. American. Late
18th century. 40" x 108".
The design is painted, yellow
and brown lozenges on canvas,
an old American favorite.
                Fig.625

THEOREM PAINTING, 1808-1860, the best period having been from 1820-1860. Found on velvet and paper, sometimes on linen and silk. A theorem is one of many stencils making a picture. Sometimes called an "Indian Tint" or a "Poonah Painting." Paint was applied with small stiff brushes called "scrubs," through stencils. Sometimes a velvet finger was used.

THEOREM PAINTING. American. 1808-1860. Red and green. At the right is one of the stencils used for the painting at the left.   Fig.626

VALENTINE THEOREM. 1835-1840, on paper. Fig.626A

<u>THEOREM PAINTED PICTURE</u> on velvet.
Fig.627

<u>THEOREM PAINTED</u> belt, on velvet. 26" x 1 1/2" wide.
Fig.628

<u>THEOREM PAINTED HAND SCREEN</u>, or
face screen, on velvet. 1800's.
8" handle, 10 1/2" x 8" screen.
Fig.629

<u>WINDOW SHADES</u>

Window shades were manufactured as early as 1830 and were
popular through 1860. In a much degraded fashion they
could be found as late as 1900. They were sold by itinerant peddlers, ready made, in sets or pairs, and by the
bolt, with an appropriate design on sized muslin. Spe-
ial orders were carried out for customers so desiring.
In 1840 they were sold along the Mississippi River and
along the Ohio. The designs were appropriate for steam-
boats, shops, even for undertaker parlors. The most
popular decoration was floral bouquets, fancy and landscape borders, Gothic windows, romantic and oriental landscapes painted in transparent oil colors.

PAINTED WINDOW SHADE. American.
1830-1860.   Fig.630

PENWORK

Pen work, in which the patterns were reversed in (usually black) paintwork to show the light-colored background, was a common form of decoration in England in the 19th century. Occasionally bright colors, notably green and red, were introduced as well and sometimes the work was executed on white or cream-colored (painted) backgrounds. While the details were carried out with a pen, larger areas were painted with a brush. Although it was usually quite small objects that were decorated in this technique, tables and small cabinets were also embellished in this manner. When done on natural wood (most popular), the design was drawn with pen and ink. Occasionally red and green paint was added. Sometimes the background was painted cream or in light colors, in which case the design was done with a brush and ink; smaller details with a pen. See Figures 345 and 359.

SCANDINAVIAN DESIGN

Norwegian "rosmaling," or rose painting, is essentially a rustic art of the country districts, found on walls, ceilings, and furniture, and on small objects such as ale bowls, caskets, jugs, and chests. "Rose painting" means the stylized reproduction of roses and other flowers, plus rustic painting in general with its figures, geometric patterns, scrolls, sometimes landscapes. The Norwegian peasant loved color and ornamentation. Kroting or chalk decoration, an early expression, is found mostly on ceilings. 1750-1850.

ROSE PAINTING (ROSMALING). A door panel, circa 1800, with
a typical Telemark rose (root, stem, leaves, and flower)
in red, white, salmon, lavender, and blue rose, white
root, shades of blue in the scrolls, on a green background.
                                                    Fig.631

DESIGN TECHNIQUES

As Practiced by Members of

The Historical Society of Early American Decoration

It was Esther Stevens Brazer who revived the old techniques of Early American Decoration and of the English decoration as practiced in the late 18th and early 19th centuries in the Midlands and in Pontypool, Wales. It was probably also she who gave the name "Chippendale painting" to the painting found on the old English Gothic trays recorded and reproduced today. The same applies, in all probability, to the term "lace-edge painting." The creation of a design, even an entire picture, in bronze powders on a tacky surface became known colloquially as "freehand bronzing," and the painting on American tin of the nineteenth century became "country painting."

After Esther Stevens Brazer's death, eighty of her pupils formed the Esther Stevens Brazer Guild which, as it grew, was granted a charter and became today's Historical Society of Early American Decoration, Inc. These members, many of whom followed in Mrs. Brazer's footsteps to become teachers and dedicated researchers, carried on and perfected the techniques already revived, further developing them. There follows a definition of these techniques. The illustrations in this glossary show, to a fairly complete extent, on what sort of objects they were used.

CHIPPENDALE PAINTING. A style of decorative painting in which realistic flowers and leaves are formed in their base coats of opaque and/or semi-opaque paint, then painted with transparent paints -- called floating colors -- then accented with white. It has a translucent, irridescent quality. The flower painting is frequently framed by gold-leaf scrolls, (metal leaf) arabesques, and drips. Sometimes the background is bronzed in a cloud effect. Birds, peacocks, and birds of paradise, painted over gold leaf (metal leaf), and fountains are further typical features of this type tray. The name applied to this type of painting, probably by Mrs. Brazer, has nothing to do

with Chippendale furniture or style. Chippendale painting
is found on gothic trays, rectangle trays, snuffers, bread
baskets, card trays, sides, lap desks, articles of furniture, boxes, etc, on metal, papier mache, and wood.

COUNTRY PAINTING. Brush-stroke patterns on furniture, wood,
and tinware. Pendant brush strokes (tassels), swags, tear-
drops, etc. Narrow patterns for flanges. Stems added to
stylized flowers, showing the way they grow. Leaves fill
in the pattern. Lastly, overstrokes and details painted
on leaves and flowers. The tin painters used white for
highlights and alizarin crimson for dark shadows.

The different American states where country tin was painted have a few typical characteristics:

Some examples of COUNTRY PAINTING brush strokes. Fig.632

Connecticut: geometric patterns and white bands.

Maine: heart-shaped leaves; black, red, and yellow backgrounds, no white bands, wet-in-wet painting, platform
top and flat top trunks. The pieces themselves vary
somewhat from those made in Connecticut.

New York: the design tends to go from left to right.
Red bands, green overstrokes, red stems, green flower
centers, bulbous bonnet-type flowers, white, yellow, and
red veins in the leaves, red fruit with yellow thumb
smudging and little black dots.

Pennsylvania: browns, siennas, blues, odd colors. Black
tendrils and veins. Crystallized backgrounds and lots of
red grounds. Thin white circles with overpainting. Many
white bands. Thumb work.

This by no means covers all types found, nor the over-
lapping of designs due to the moving of tinsmiths and
painters from place to place.

FREEHAND BRONZING. A method of decoration practiced in
England in the 18th and 19th centuries. Bronze powders
are applied freehand (not through a stencil) with small
dry brushes and stumps into a tacky varnish surface to
form the design which may be flowers, fruit, animals, in-
sects, scenic themes, etc.

LACE-EDGE PAINTING. A style of decoration associated
with the pierced-edge trays of Pontypool (also used on
other ware). The designs were flowers, fruit, birds,
etc. which show great depth of form by a contrast of
deep shadow with strongly textured highlights and white
or off-white accents. The early trays usually had a
tortoise-shell background with floral sprays around a
central motif, sometimes an Adam-style urn. Impasto
was used to give relief and a third dimensional quality. The veining, gold leaf, and striping were very fine.
The name "lace-edge painting" probably originated with

Mrs. Brazer, also the designation of "lace-edge" tray
for those on which such work was found, reflecting the
lacy effect of the pierced edging.

METAL LEAF WORK. The design is applied to the object
in a varnish medium, and gold, silver, or copper leaf
is laid into this tacky varnish when almost dry. Surplus leaf is then brushed away from the edges. If the
design requires it, form is given by etching the metal
leaf, and depth is created by washes of umber paint.
Beautiful effects are sometimes achieved by the use of
different shades of metal leaf in the same design.

DESIGN TECHNIQUES ON GLASS

METAL LEAF ON GLASS. The metal leaf is laid in gelatin
and water size on the back of the glass. The design is
etched on the metal leaf, then backed with black paint
or asphaltum. After the surplus leaf has been washed
away, the rest of the glass is painted.

REVERSE PAINTING ON GLASS. The process of painting is
done on the back of the glass and therefore reversed,
i.e. the details which seem to be on top are done first,
all backgrounds last. May also be called "back" painting.

REVERSE PAINTING ON GLASS and stenciling for a clock tablet. Plymouth,
Connecticut. 1880. 8" x 10". A
cavalier, painted, on horseback. Stenciled peaches and strawberries in
the corners. Possibly done by Mr.
Fenn whose daughter also painted clock
dials and tablets. The little cavalier is typical of their designs.

                              Fig.633

REVERSE PAINTING AND STENCILING ON GLASS. So-called Jenny
Lind glasses. Named after the Swedish singer who was so
popular in this country. She visited Birmingham in 1849
and traveled in this country with P. T. Barnum from 1850
to 1852. We have no authentication for where these glasses
were painted, but they are found mainly in looking glasses.
                                                Fig.634

REVERSE PAINTING ON GLASS. A country scene, reverse painted, with a stenciled border. Typical Empire looking-glass
tablet.   Fig.635

REVERSE PAINTING ON GLASS. Architectural type with gold-leaf border, and gold-leaf border around pendulum hole, all on the reverse side of glass. Typical Terry clock tablet.   Fig.636

STENCILING. The art of applying bronze powders through cut-out patterns to a tacky varnished surface.   Fig.637A

STENCILING, "PIANO". The so-called "piano" stenciling is the same as the above, but a combination with free-hand bronze is also used.   Fig.637B

STENCILING, WALLS OR FLOORS.   Oil (japan) or water paints are used through a stencil onto a dry and un-varnished surface by means of velvet, chamois, brushes, etc.   Fig.637C

TRANSFER PICTURES on glass (also found on wood, metal, ceramics, etc.) may be traced back to the late years of Charles II (1630-1701). They were at their zenith from 1750-1770. Briefly, a transfer picture on glass is the black print of a mezzotint engraving cemented to the reverse side of a piece of glass and colored by hand after removal of the paper pulp from the back of the print. The declining years were 1780-1810.

Mezzotints, used as a basis for old glass pictures, were introduced to England by Prince Rupert who bought the working details from the inventor, Ludwig von Giegen, circa 1665.

Balloon Assention. 1787-

The engraved print plus the painter's art results in what is known as "mezzotinto" prints on glass. Handbooks sometimes refer to the craft as "behind coloring." See also Fig.387 and 389.   Fig.638

DECORATED WALLS AND FLOORS

The wall and floor painters of the late 18th and early 19th centuries were mostly itinerants who covered a lot of territory, finding many customers eager to have their walls and floors decorated in "the new fashion." Free-hand painted walls and floors were soon followed by stenciling with paint directly on the plaster or wood. Some of the old stencils in their original kits, complete with paints and brushes, have been found and are a boon to the researcher in studying his designs. There are characterizations to each decorator's work, the colors he favored, the placement of the design, and the manner in which it

was applied to floors and walls. Unfortunately most of
the work on floors and walls still remains anonymous.
We have chosen two wall decorators who are known, probably
the most renowned, the one a stenciler, the other primar-
ily a painter: Moses Eaton and Rufus Porter. See also
the entries for these artists under "Painters and Craftsmen."

WALL STENCILS.   Five typical Moses Eaton wall stencils.
See page 269.   Fig.639A-E

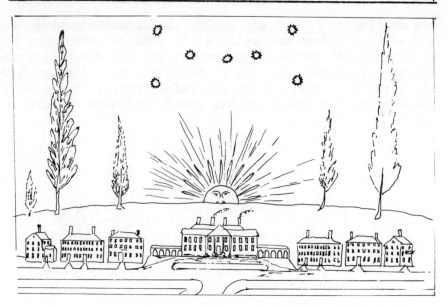

Overmantel painting of Dartmouth College, Hanover, New
Hampshire, by Rufus Porter. It hangs over the mantel of
the central fireplace, Prescott Tavern, East Jaffrey, New
Hampshire. Circa 1824. See page 278.   Fig.640

PAINTERS
and
CRAFTSMEN

ALSAGER, JOHN. Apprenticed at Jennens and Bettridge (Birmingham). Was well known as a painter in the oriental style. He entered into partnership with George Neville in 1846. They developed, among other things, a method of pearl shell inlay which differed from others in that no painting or tinting of the shell was involved. See Fig. 280.

BARKER, BENJAMIN. Born in Pontypool circa 1740, died 1793. An itinerant sporting artist, Barker was engaged as foreman decorator during the mid-1760's at Pontypool. Coats of arms on trays have been attributed to him. He used Chinese themes combined with applied metal ornament in the current Adam style. It has also been said that he introduced flower painting in a style known at the time as "Van Huysum" flowers. (Jan Van Huysum was a Dutch painter famous for his flower paintings, 1682-1749). Barker was succeeded as foreman painter and copyist circa 1790 by Thomas Pemberton of the Old Hall Works, Wolverhampton. Barker (Benjamin) was the father of the eminent artists Benjamin Barker, Jr. and Thomas Barker. The Barker family moved to Bath when the boys were young.

BARKER, BENJAMIN, JR. 1776-1838. Son of Benjamin Barker, he learned his art in Pontypool and it is said that he decorated some of their finest trays. He was basically an animal painter but also excelled in landscapes.

BARKER, THOMAS. 1770-1847. Born in Pontypool, son of Benjamin, and older brother of Benjamin, Jr. In 1793 he was painting rustic scenes and figures of shepherds and woodsmen. These paintings were copied profusely. The ones we find on tin are probably copies. He was the popular painter of his day and was called "Barker of Bath." See Fig.57 and 260.

BARNEY, JOSEPH. 1751-1827. Decorator. After 27 years as drawing master at the Royal Academy in Woolwich, he returned to Wolverhampton to paint trays for his brother, a partner in the firm of Bevins & Barney. He was well known as a tray painter of religious subjects. His painted classical and scriptural subjects for altar pieces still decorate several Staffordshire churches.   See Fig.180.

BARNHART, JOHN. 1760-1810. He ornamented Baltimore furniture for the Thomas Renshaw furniture company in that
city. See Fig.555.

BOOTH, JOSEPH. Painter, introduced a style of oriental
design while working at Jennens & Bettridge in Birmingham
from 1821 to 1835. His design known as the "willow pattern"
was formal and conventional to a degree. It was widely
copied and imitated at other manufactories. Booth and his
copyists gave their human faces a Western cast. He worked
in gesso relief, gold leaf, and bronze powders. His personal work, sometimes signed, is found only on papier-mâché.

BUCKLEY, OLIVER. 1781-1872. Trained in Berlin, Connecticut, moved to Stevens Plains, Maine, at the age of four-
teen, became a smith and painter. His designs were geometric, with simple brush strokes. Another characteristic
of his was the use of a main design painted with an orange
or salmon pink base. He took Walter B. Goodrich into the
business, 1824-1825, and again from 1837-1842.

BUTLER FAMILY. In 1799 Abel Butler moved his family from
Connecticut to Greenville, New York. His son, Aaron, was
sent to Berlin, Connecticut, to learn tinsmithing. In
1824 he opened a tin shop and store in Greenville. Of
Aaron's ten children, Ann, Minerva, and Marilla are known
to have painted tinware. The tinshop closed in 1859 and
Aaron died in 1860. See Fig.246.

BUTLER, ANN. Born in 1813. She managed her father's
shop until her marriage in 1835. In 1843 John Miller,
who had married her sister, Minerva, took over this re-
sponsibility. Ann was one of the few decorators who
signed her work, sometimes with her full name, sometimes
with her initials only, which were often encased in a
heart made of yellow brush strokes. The initials were
formed with a series of dots. It is believed that Ann
taught her sisters.

BUTLER, MINERVA. Born in 1821. An autograph album illustrated by Minerva, with the same sort of designs

found on the Butler tinware, confirms pieces done by the
Butler sisters. The designs were very busy, with few
bare spots. Rick-rack (zig-zag), dots, brush strokes,
star-shaped flowers, rose buds, tulips, and unusual leaf
treatment were typical of Butler ornamentation. There
are some known family pieces, however, which have a
different flavor. They are simpler in design and thought
to be done for the trade by the shop. This has been con-
firmed by the finding of many such pieces in other shops
and ownership outside the family. Pieces have been
found signed: "Minerva," in writing, and "M.B." which
could have been Minerva or Marilla.

CLAY, HENRY. See entries under INVENTORS & INVENTIONS
and under MANUFACTURERS & MANUFACTORIES.

COOK, RANSOM. 1794-1854. Furniture maker and stenciler,
he opened a shop in Saratoga Springs, N.Y. in 1813. Business prospered, and in 1827-1828 he built a new home
and factory on South Broadway. He was known for the
geometric arrangement of his designs and was an exceed-
ingly fine stenciler. Some of his stencils were found
in an old account book and are now in the collection of
the Saratoga Springs Historical Society. See Fig. 347
& 482.

CROSSMAN, ROBERT. 1707-1799. From 1724-1740 furniture
and drum maker. Famous as maker and decorator of Taunton chests at Taunton, Massachusetts. He created the
vine-tree of life design on brown or natural wood, later
added bird and tulip motifs. See Fig.538.

CURTIS, LEMUEL. 1790-1857. Worked in Concord, Massachusetts from 1814-1818, then in Burlington, Vermont until his death. For a time he was associated with Mr.
Dunning, a clockmaker. His most important clock was
called the "Curtis" clock. It was quite similar to the
banjo clock, except for the round lower frame. It is
perhaps the most beautiful of all American clocks. Although it has no candle arms, it was sometimes called
the "girandole" clock, since the pendulum has a circular frame, studded with gilt balls resembling the girandole looking glass in shape and design. The convex

glass of the pendulum box had a reverse-glass painting
and was flanked with brass sidearms. The clock has a
gilt eagle finial. We occasionally come across one
with a thermometer framed in delicate painting, which
is not a true Curtis clock. See entry under CLOCKS and
also Fig. 409 & 410.

CUTTING & MORRILL. Chair stencilers and painters. Their
shop was listed in the 1851-1852 Directory for Albany,
New York at 13 Church Street. Some of their stencils
have been preserved in the Metropolitan Museum of Art,
New York. See Fig.453.

DAVIS, WILLIAM. Decorator in the English Midlands, probably Wolverhampton. Circa 1817 he adopted a method of
decorating which created a picture with various bronze
powders on trays with a dark background, using bobs or
small chamois tools, without the use of opaque pigment.
His designs were scriptural or allegorical. He also
copied George Morland's rustic subjects to perfection.
After working at Wolverhampton, he moved to Birmingham,
dying as an old man in the McCallum and Hodgson shop.

EATON, MOSES, Sn. 1753-1833 and son EATON, MOSES, Jr.
1796-about 1856. Itinerant wall stencilers. Jr. was
born in Hancock, New Hampshire, moved later to Harris-
ville, which is part of Dublin, New Hampshire. Although it is said that he turned to farming after his
marriage, there are many walls in New Hampshire, Massachusetts and Maine that have patterns he was known to
have used. Along with his father, according to family
tradition, he used the wall stencil kit. In this stencil kit, now preserved in the museum of the Society for
the Preservation of New England Antiquities, are eight
brushes and seventy-eight stencils that make up forty
complete designs for walls and chairs. Judging by the
amount of paint on the stencils, his favorites or most
used were an oak leaf, a large flower spray, a diagon-
al border, a rose and leaf. Note Fig.639.

EATON, WILLIAM PAGE. 1819-1904. Chair painter of Boston, born in Salem, Massachusetts. Following his second

marriage in 1843 he lived for a short time in Chelsea, Massachusetts and in New Bedford, Massachusetts. He returned to Boston in 1845, where he opened a shop in Fulton Street. Called "the best of the New England stencilers" by George Lord of Portland, Maine. William Eaton was a leading decorator from the 1840's on. He trained and worked in the Boston area but later moved to his farm between Boston and South Weare, New Hampshire where he continued to practice his craft. His workmanship surpassed that of other craftsmen in grace and skill during this late period. He often painted roses in the center of a chair design, surrounding them with delicate and graceful stenciled scrolls, sometimes signing his name within the decoration. As fashions changed and walnut furniture supplanted stenciled and painted chairs, Eaton turned to farming. See Fig.452.

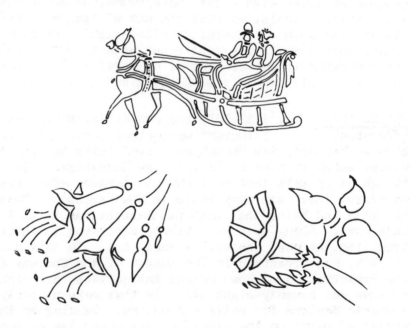

W. P. Eaton signature and stencils. Fig.641A-D

W. P. Eaton stencil.   Fig.641E

FENN, WILLIAM BENNET. 1813-1890, Plymouth, Connecticut.
A fine painter and stenciler of clocks. He had a daughter, Mrs. Mary E. Stephenson, who followed in his footsteps. She died in the 1950's. One of their clock tablets is "The Little Cavalier," a child on a pony with
leaves and peaches in the corners of the stenciled glass,
another name, perhaps for "The Young Cavalier" shown in
Fig.633. From 1840-1853 Fenn worked almost continuously
for Seth Thomas, although in his early years he worked
for a number of clock makers. In 1864 he married his
chief helper, Mary Culver.

GILDERSLEEVE, THOMAS JEFFERSON. 1805-1871. He was a
"Gilder" and a "Maker of Furniture and Chairs of all
Descriptions" according to his trade card. In 1820 he
came to New York from Springfield, New Jersey to become
apprenticed to Richard Tweed, chairmaker and family
friend and father of "Boss" Tweed. In 1827 Gildersleeve
opened his own shop on Delancy Street. When his house
and shop were razed, he opened a shop at 197 Chatham
Street, together with a fellow craftsman named Madden.
He retired in 1861. Some of his stencil powders and
tools, including his handmade stencil knife and etcher,
have survived along with more than forty stencils which
were found in an old family scrapbook. The stencils
were the type used on chairs from 1820 on. Unfortunately two known Gildersleeve chairs were stripped and

refinished in the 1930's, and no other known examples
have come to light. Fig.481 shows what might be an example of his work.

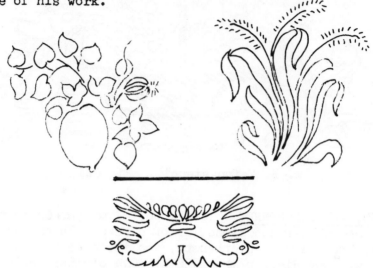

Gildersleeve stencils, circa 1830.   Fig.642A-C

GILLAM, CHARLES. Saybrook, Connecticut. Furniture
joiner, strongly believed by collectors and antiquarians to have made the Guilford painted chests. This is
based on an inventory in the Guilford Probate Records
dated August 23, 1727. The list consisted of a number
of cabinet makers tools, "Chest of drawers not finished, frame for chest of drawers, painted chest with drawers, a parcel of collours, boxes, brushes, and gums.
109 lbs. oaker & umber," and on the fact that Charles
was certainly trained by a 17th century furniture joiner. See Fig.535.

GOODRICH, WALTER B. See entry under "Buckley, Oliver,"
page 267.

HANCOCK, ROBERT. Engraver, circa 1756. His engraved
designs were freely adapted and executed from Jean
Pillement's designs, some from The Ladies Amusement,
and after C. Fenn's birds. Undoubtedly his shell patterns came from the same source. See Fig.241.

HASELAR, EDWIN. He is believed to have introduced real-
ism into "flowering." He and George Neville worked together so closely in point of time, place, and style
that it is impossible to tell their work apart. Between
them they raised the art to unparalleled heights. Haselar lived to be ninety and was always employed by others.
He worked for Jennens & Bettridge in Birmingham from 1832-
1845/46, after which he moved to Walton's in London and
had six apprentices. This helped him financially, since
he received a royalty for every copy of his designs sold.
About 1850 Frederick Walton employed Edwin Haselar to
paint the flowers in the center of a fine papier-mâché
tea tray to give to Her Majesty Queen Victoria, who was
to pass through Wolverhampton on a certain day. Walton
gave Haselar the latest specimen of roses for his models.
He was a great realistic flower painter. The day came
and the tray was laden with the finest hot-house grapes,
and when the tray was passed into the carriage the
grapes were swept onto a table and the tray was handed
back through the window of the starting train! This
embittered Edwin's life for a long time.

HINKS, JAMES. Decorator in Birmingham, England. Created the Persian style of tray ornamentation in 1855, a
vogue that lasted for approximately five years. The designs resembled those found on Persian carpets; gold
outlined vari-shaped spaces which were filled in with
bright colors. He worked for McCallum & Hodgson. See
Fig.226.

HITCHCOCK. See entry under MANUFACTURERS & MANUFACTOR-
IES, also Fig.462, 463, 464, 466 and 479.

JACKSON, WILLIAM. Decorator, Wolverhampton. Among
other things, painted lilies-of-the-valley on bellows,
blotters, and diverse small articles. Also may be recognized by the following border:

Fig.643

His lilies were copied and were soon badly executed.
His motifs of heather, heath and fern (before 1860) were
also popular with copyists.

JOHNSON (or JOHNSTON), THOMAS, see REA & JOHNSTON, p. 278.

JONES, WILLIAM H., and brothers. Wolverhampton, 1853-
1896. They were prominent japanners, mostly on household
goods such as bedsteads, coal scuttles, deed boxes, or tin
trunks. The brothers were apprenticed at F. Walton's
shop where their father was a foreman for 25 years. See
Fig.89.

KAUFFMAN, ANGELICA. 1741-1807. A Swiss historical and
portrait painter. After studying in Italy, she went to
London and became famous for classical and mythological
paintings. In 1766 she executed ceilings and murals designed by Robert Adam. Her husband was Antonio Zucchi,
also a painter and decorator under the auspices of the
Adam brothers. See Fig.571.

LEHN, JOSEPH. 1798-1892. Decorator on wood. Worked
from 1860-1886. Painted chairs, buckets, tubs, water
kegs, seed or spice chests, cups and saucers, sugar
stands, egg cups, saffron boxes, salt cellars, sewing
boxes, toys and penny banks. His favorite motifs were
the strawberry, a pomegranate-like object, and pussy
willow borders. A yellow stripe, 1/16", is typical,
simulating paneling or emphasizing the form of the piece
or its decoration. Buckets were grained in reddish
ochre over a yellow ground. See Fig.371-375.

LORD, GEORGE. 1833-1928. Called by Janet Waring and
Esther Stevens Brazer "the last of the old chair stencilers." From Portland, Maine. He painted and stenciled
chairs from his fifteenth to his eighty-seventh year, and
to the end was using stenciled patterns of seventy years'
standing. To Esther Stevens Brazer he was an invaluable
source of information on the art of stenciling.

MOORE, WILLIAM, Jr. Born in 1765 in Barkhamsted. Date
of death unknown. Two chairs have been found that were
signed by him. These were possibly decorated circa 1824.

Since one bears a design almost identical to a design
popular at the Lambert Hitchcock factory, William Moore,
Jr. may have worked for Hitchcock. He was working in
Barkhamsted about 1790, but went out of business in 1839.

Stenciled slat of the William Moore, Jr. chair, very similar to one made by L. Hitchcock. See Fig.476. Fig.644

MORLAND, GEORGE. 1763-1804. English painter of rustic
scenes and animals, who exhibited sketches at the Royal
Academy at the age of ten. A dissolute life marred a
career that might have been exceptional. In the last
eight years of his life he turned out 492 pictures for
his brother, who became the middleman between him and
his customers and creditors. Many of his best works have
been preserved by engravers in mezzotints. Copyists
found his paintings highly adaptable and popular when reproduced on trays. See Fig.134 & 213.

NEVILLE, GEORGE. 1810-1887. Decorator and painter, apprenticed to Jennens & Bettridge at an early age. After
a trip to Paris in 1830 he developed a new technique of
painting flowers naturalistically, on a black background.
Before this a bronzed background had been generally used.
He was fond of painting parrots and birds of paradise.
There is a fine transparency about his rose petals, which
is unmistakable, for it is possible to see through one
petal to another. He painted the morning glory with a
folded or turned-up edge, showing a fragment of the reverse in another color, rather than a straight forward
round blue flower. He painted down to the black background. For some years, before leaving Jennens & Bettridge, he was foreman there and had pupils working under
him, some of whom became distinguished in their own right
In 1846 he joined forces with John Alsager and they formed the company of Alsager & Neville. They produced many

blanks and decorated the borders on them, which were
subsequently finished by other firms. They also evolved
a method of shell inlay which was different from others
in that the shell was neither tinted nor painted. Neville painted very few articles after 1850. See Fig.280.

NORTH, MERCY. Fly Creek, New York. Her dates are about
1798-1838. Decorator. Daughter of Stephen North who
was proprietor of a tin shop from circa 1790. A signed
bun basket exists, with several borders of expert brush
strokes, the red strokes fat and full. The background
has zig-zag black graining on asphaltum, typical of her
work, as are her white and red bands. There are many
other pieces with the same characteristics, white bands,
red bands, red, green, and yellow brush strokes around
a handle. With eight brothers and sisters, we find Albert and Linus and at least two of Albert's sons listed
as tinsmiths, also a second wife of "Norris North, Tinsmith," called "Mercy North," from Elmira, New York.

PEMBERTON, THOMAS. See entry under "Barker, B." p.266.

PENNIMAN, JOHN RITTO. Boston, Massachusetts. Born in
mid-eighteenth century, died probably in the first quarter of the nineteenth century, he studied with the famous

Dressing box, bird's-eye maple, circa 1800. Boston.
Thought to be decorated by John R. Penniman.   Fig.645A

American painter Benjamin West (1738-1820) and traveled
with Gilbert Stuart (1755-1828). He painted the fine
shell decoration on the Salem Sheraton swell-front chest
of drawers now in the Museum of Fine Arts in Boston.
The fine cross-hatching on Fig.408B is by him, a gold-
leaf lattice pattern in reverse painting. As far as we
know, none of this work was carried on after Penniman's
death.

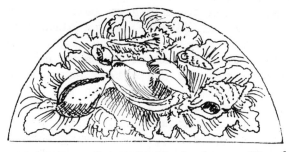

A typical Penniman shell design.   Fig.645B.

PERGOLESI, MICHEL ANGELO. Italian artist. He arrived
in England circa 1770 and worked for Robert Adam as a
painter of walls, ceilings, furniture, etc. in the
classical manner. He also published original designs
of painted motifs.

PILLEMENT, JEAN-BAPTISTE. 1719-1808. A French artist
and designer, a meticulous and prolific worker whose designs were published in several volumes. He is credited
with the invention of "chinoiseries." Born in Lyons,
France, he worked in Paris and London. His work is
largely imaginary and based to a great extent on oriental
influences. Many of his designs contained Chinese fountains, Chinese tents, "Persian" flowers, all of which

From The Ladies Amusement or The Whole Art of Japanning
made Easy, by Robert Sayer.   Fig.646

were copied by the decorators and japaners of his day.
In the Ladies Amusement, published in 1760, there are
some thirty-nine patterns, a good example of his work,
among others.

PORTER, RUFUS (1792-1884). Inventor of water wheels,
windmills, lathes, etc. and a musician -- he played
the fife and violin -- and a poet. In 1810 he became
apprenticed to a house and sign painter. At the out-
break of the War of 1812 he was painting gunboats and
playing the fife for the Portland Light Infantry. He
also painted sleighs, taught drumming and wrote books.
Around 1815 he started his career as an itinerant portrait painter, but the inventor in him would not die.
Between 1820 and 1840 he worked on various labor-saving
devices such as a corn sheller, churn, washing machine,
steam carriage, an alarm, a revolving almanac, many of
which inventions he sold outright. In 1824 he started
his "Landscape Painting on Walls," which was a huge
success. His book, "Curious Arts," went into five editions. In 1840 he decided to become a newspaper editor;
this was followed by an electroplating venture and another invention -- a revolving rifle which he sold to
Col. Samuel Colt for $100 -- the now famous Colt revol-
ver! Hale and hearty to the last three days of his
life, he died while visiting his son in New Haven, Connecticut at the age of ninety-three.

REA & JOHNSTON. Thomas Johnston, or Johnston of Boston,
(1708-1767) was an able japanner skilled in ornamenting
clocks and furniture with embossed or raised work re-
presenting Chinese figures. He also painted coats-of-
arms and from 1746 was an engraver. His four sons --
Thomas (1731-   ), William (1732-   ), Benjamin (1740-
1818) and John (1753-   ) were painters, and except
for William, also japanners. In 1764 Daniel Rea II, a
japanner, married Rachel Johnston, a sister, and when
Thomas died, took over the business. In 1773 John became a partner, and as Rea & Johnston they carried on
the business which, in spite of competition, was responsible for a large part of the decorating done in Boston
from 1750 to 1800. Their work was similar to that shown
in Fig.544.

SCHIMMEL, WILLIAM. 1817-1890. A Pennsylvanian whose
carvings are distinguished by their vigor and the sub-
tlety with which they portray the essence of each animal or bird he carved. His eagles are not simply por-
traits of the bird, they seem to personify the whole
category of eagle characteristics. He also carved and
painted tigers, squirrels, dogs, and lions. He would
exchange his carvings for a night's lodgings, a meal, or
a glass of rum. He died penniless after producing
approximately five hundred memorable pieces of wood carving. See Fig.378 & 379.

SELTZER, CHRISTIAN. 1747-1831. From Jonestown, Lebanon
County, Pennsylvania. Although he depended on farming
and innkeeping for his livelihood, his greatest interest
lay in painting dowry chests which have been found dated
from 1771 to 1796. His chests vary greatly since he was
constantly experimenting with design. After 1790 his
painting became more graceful, with better proportions,
delicacy, and refinement. His level of craftsmanship
was never equalled by his contemporaries. See Fig.530.

SELTZER, JOHN. 1774-1845. Son of Christian Seltzer,
painted in the style of his father from 1800 to 1810.
See Fig.531.

STEVENS, ZACHARIAH BRACKETT. Stevens Plains, Maine.
Opened his shop in 1798. In 1830 he turned it over to
his sons. His designs were imaginative and quite unique. The leaves and flowers were blended with two or
more colors -- so-called "wet-on-wet" painting. Cherries as a motif were frequently used. Fine cross-hatching of flower centers was another characteristic. His
yellow brush-stroke borders were bright and the sides
of his tin trunks had, as a rule, three or four yellow
strokes forming a small circle. In April, 1842, fire
destroyed the shops of Zachariah and Samuel Stevens.
See Fig.41, 50, 248, & 249.

STOBWASSER, JOHANN HEINRICH. German japanner, born in
1740, was the son of a peddler. He learned the business
of lacquering in Ansbach, and decorated swagger sticks,
belts, munitions canisters, mugs, boxes, and trinkets.

In 1760 he became acquainted with English lacquering and
from 1763 revolutionized the Brunswick lacquer trade,
which had been lagging behind that of Berlin and Dresden,
Germany, and was anxious to compete successfully with
Birmingham. From then on he worked on papier-mâché and
tin, painting figures, landscapes, an enterprise in which
he was joined by his entire family. They decorated
pipes, snuff boxes, mugs, cups, trays, table tops, pots,
now and then a coffee table or bureau. During his lifetime his workers left to establish firms of their own
all over Germany and into Bohemia. After 1775 his work
was stamped with his mark -- a horse over an "ST," or
was signed "Stobwasser Fabrik." See Fig.172.

THOMAS, JOHN. A landscape artist who painted for Jennens & Bettridge, Birmingham, between 1830 and 1850.
See Fig.278.

WALLIS, GEORGE. 1811-1891. Worked as a painter at B.
Walton's in Wolverhampton. He designed and painted the
Victoria Tray, an oval tray with a scalloped edge (1838).
See Fig.201. He became a recognized artist and an author-
ity in his field.

INVENTORS
and
INVENTIONS

ALLGOOD, THOMAS. 1655-1716. He and his eldest son, Edward, 1681-1763, developed a tinning process and began japanning the metal to compete with the "oriental" products in Pontypool. The "secret" of Pontypool japanning was an application of linseed oil varnishes which had been oxidized and were made permanent with heat when the pieces were fired in ovens. The first objects made were so-called "waiters" (round trays), candlesticks, tobacco and snuff boxes, chestnut urns, teapots, and caddies.

BARBER, GEORGE. Bilston, England. In 1834 he invented the art of transferring designs to trays, a method universally adapted later for the decoration of cheaper goods. At the height of his prosperity, Barber, along with other Bilston firms, exported 50,000 picture trays, tea caddies, etc. weekly. After 1850 cork was used for printing borders and the centers of trays both by him and by his son-in-law, Richard Lawkey. See CORK PRINTING and TRANSFER PRINTING, pages 283 and 284.

BASKERVILLE, JOHN. 1706-1775. English printer. While at Birmingham he made some important improvements in the process of japanning. Later he experimented with paper. Henry Clay worked for Baskerville, who greatly advanced the art of printing. His wife, Sarah, carried on his printing business for some years after his death.

BRUNSON (or BRONSON), OLIVER. A master tinsmith who made unusual pieces for Oliver Filley, including the crooked-spout coffee pot. He was with Filley from 1800 to 1822, and was at the shop in Elizabethtown, New Jersey, in 1810, and in the Simsbury, Connecticut, shop in 1814. Plain tinware was often sent from Filley's shops to other parts of the country to be decorated and sold. A Brunson-Filley crooked-spout coffee pot could easily appear in Pennsylvania, with Pennsylvania decoration. Brunson, however, was active mainly in Connecticut and New Jersey.

CLAY, HENRY. In 1772 he took out a patent for the manufacture of boards or panels of papier-mâché. See the CLAY entry in the section on "Manufacturers and Manufactories."

CORK PRINTING. An invention attributed to Barber and
Lawley. Cork was used for printing after 1850 by a
method resembling linoleum-block printing. A single
motif was cut in the cork, which was dipped in bronze
varnish and stamped on the borders of trays. The floors
of these trays were usually decorated with a one-unit
stencil washed with a transparent color. In a third step
a small detail was sometimes applied to the flowers by
a cut cork dipped in paint.

DAGUERRE, LOUIS JACQUES MANDÉ. 1789-1851. A French
painter and physicist who in 1839 introduced the first
photographic picture or "daguerreotype," on which he
had collaborated with the French inventor Joseph Nice-
phore Niepce. See the DAGUERREOTYPE entry in the
"Vocabulary," page 332.

SEWING MACHINE. This is the result of varied inventions
by numerous inventors. The first one to really work was
patented by Barthelemy Thimmonier of St. Étienne, France,
in 1830. He died in 1857 after his patent rights for
Great Britain were sold. The eye-point needle and the
lock-stitch were American inventions conceived by Walter
Hunt of New York, circa 1832-1834. Hunt was an important inventor but reaped no reward. His invention was
bought by a Mr. Arrowsmith who did a good deal to im-
prove mechanical details. Soon machines were developed
based on the Hunt invention, but he was unable to get a
patent on the grounds of abandonment. Hunt's eye-point
needle was patented in 1841 by Newton and Archbold in the
United Kingdom. Elias Howe of Spencer, Massachusetts,
patented a rough model in 1846 and sold it the same year
to William F. Thomas of London, who took out the patent
in his own name and hired E. Howe on weekly wages to
adapt the machine to his manufacturing purposes. Along
came Isaac Merritt Singer, 1811-1875, who secured a
patent for his machine in 1851. Mr. Howe, feeling his
rights were infringed upon, brought suit. Ultimately
all makers became tributary to E. Howe, who died in 1867,
one month after receiving not less than two million dol-
lars in the form of royalties. Wheeler & Wilson(1849),
Grover & Baker (1851), and Wilcox & Gibbs (1856), all

American inventors, together produced the machines now
in common use. See Fig.131 & 132.

TIN PRINTING. This was introduced about 1875. It is the
application of the lithographic processes to the decoration of metal plate. (Lithography means "stone writing.")
In the original process, prints were made directly from
designs drawn on slabs of stone. The principal is that
oil and water do not mix. The design is outlined on the
printing surface with a greasy substance. Water is applied to the printing surface. The water is repelled
by the grease but adheres to the non-greasy areas. Ink
is then applied. The ink sticks to the grease but not
to the wet areas. The ink is then transferred to the
paper.

The invention of the power press in 1865 led to the development of tin printing. The original stone press had one
cylinder, but the offset press used in tin printing has
three cylinders. The printed image is first transferred
from a plate (or stone) to a rubber blanket, then to the
tin which travels through an impression cylinder. This
prepared tin receives an impression of the design and is
then stoved in a high temperature, this being done for
each printing until all the colors to complete the design have been printed. A separate stone or plate is
required for each color.

A substantial percentage of can label work, formerly
done by paper lithographers, has in recent years gone
to the tin lithographer. Many of the metal containers
one sees, some simple, others elaborately decorated,
are the product of tin printing. This is a branch of
lithographic art in which few firms specialize. The
beautifully decorated tin containers used for confec-
tionary and household requisites are printed by this
method. This is not the same as transfer printing.
See Fig.83 and 85.

TRANSFER PRINTING. This is the method whereby patterns
printed on paper from engraved copper plates are transferred onto tin, papier-mâché, wood, etc. They were sometimes baked or "fired." See Fig.227.

Rectangular high chair tray, England, 1876. 15" x 10½".
The design is a transfer picture on a blue background.
Fig.647

VERNIS MARTIN. The name derives from a French family
of artists and "inventors." There were four brothers:
Martin-Guillaume (d.1749), Simon Étienne, Julien, and
Robert (1706-1765). They began their careers as coach
painters. They neither invented nor laid any claim to
having invented the varnish (vernis) that bears their
name, but they enormously improved and eventually
brought to perfection compositions and methods of applying the varnishes which were already familiar. Oriental
lacquer soon acquired high favor in France and many at-
tempts were made to imitate it. This varnish was very
brilliant but proved to be less durable than the oriental lacquer which had inspired it. English japanning
also surpassed it.

TINSMITHS
and
TIN CENTERS

The tin peddler.   Fig.648.

ABOUT TIN

Tin is a white malleable metallic element.   Block tin
is an impure commercial tin cast in blocks.

Tin-plate is sheet-iron plated with tin.

Tinfoil is tin rolled into very thin sheets.

Tin sheets were imported from England to Berlin, Connecticut from approximately 1750 to 1860 by the "base box,"
which was 225 sheets of common #1; 10" x 13 3/4" and 11"
x 15", called common small doubles -- C.S.D.   Size
12 1/2" x 16 3/4" was called common doubles -- C.D., and
came 100 in a box.

Tin peddler's cart.   Fig.649

The registry mark "I" stands for tin.

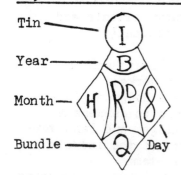

Tin ────

Year ────

Month ──

Bundle ──   Day

This all adds up to read:

Tin - 1858 - Apr 8.   Fig.650

M C ⚓ O ⚔ Ⓚ

Other tin marks. Fig.651

BILSTON. English tin center. Circa 1709. While Bilston is mentioned as the first English tin center, records are vague about its beginnings. The 1818 Registry lists 15 japanners as well as workers in the kin-
dred trades, which indicates a well-established business.
Bilston's principal products were blank trays, waiters,
bread baskets, coal vases, and trays of a cheaper type,
for export. At one time Bilston exported 50,000 trays
a week for foreign markets. Following is a list of
some of the men and women from Bilston, arranged chrono-
logically:

William Smith, 1709   Samuel Jevon, 1791
Joseph Allen, 1718   Daniel Caddick, 1791
Samuel Beckett, 1757-1803   John Peolton, 1791
John Hartell, 1781   Thomas Swindley-Stencil-
William Bickley, 1781-1798   ler, 1827
Hanson, 1781   Hannah Barratt, c.1827
Jacksons, 1781   Elizabeth Fullwood,c.1827
Homer, 1781   Jane Becket & Sons,Mfg.,
John Simmons, 1781   c.1827
Bickley and Sons, 1781   George Barber, 1834 (transfer)
Hanson and Jacks, 1781   Richard Lawley, 1850 (cork)
Joseph Barney, 1751-1826   Thomas Jones

BIRMINGHAM. English tin center. A town in the Midlands
where japanning was a staple product from just before
the middle of the 18th century until about 1860. By
1770, papier-mâché was so thoroughly established, it
was listed as a separate trade, and in due course re-
placed the production of tinware to a great extent.

Following are some of the better-known artists and
firms of Birmingham, arranged alphabetically:

Alsager & Neville
Stephen Bedford
John Baskerville
Henry Clay
G. C. Davies
Footherape, Shewell &
  Shenton
T. Farmer
Thomas Gibson (worked for
  Lane)
Halbeard & Wellings
C. P. Harris
Jennens & Bettridge

W. Lane (Great Hampton
  Street Works)
M'Cullum & Hodgson (suc-
  cessors to Jennens &
  Bettridge, and last sur-
  vivors of the industry)
Perman & Stamp
Small & Son, Guest, Chopping
  & Bill (successors to H.
  Clay)
John Taylor
Richard Turley
Charles Valentine
Watson & Co.

FILLEY, OLIVER. 1784-1846. Bloomfield and Simsbury,
Connecticut. This master tinsmith and merchant of tinware started his shop about 1800. He had branch shops
in Lansingburg, New York, managed by his cousin, Au-
gustus; in Elizabethtown, New Jersey in 1810; and in
Philadelphia, Pennsylvania, this one operated by his
brother, Harvey. In St. Louis his son Oliver Dwight
ran a shop for him. Filley shops sold nearly every
type of the finest tinware. Large yellow brush strokes
on trunk tops and sides are typical. Wet-in-wet (see
entry for STEVENS, ZACHARIAH BRACKETT under "Painters
and Craftsmen") was a technique not represented.

GERMAN TIN CENTER. Brunswick. This was a steady com-
petitor of Birmingham. Lacquerware was produced there
from the early eighteenth century. Centers in Berlin
and Dresden were equally successful. See the entry
for STOBWASSER, JOHANN HEINRICH under "Painters and
Craftsmen."

GOODRICH, WALTER B. of Stevens Plains, Maine. 1802-
1869. Kept a journal with the following facts: born May
19, 1802 at Wethersfield, Connecticut. Worked eight
months for E. A. Yale in 1823 in Lynn, Massachusetts.
Worked for Oliver Buckley in Main, 1824-1825. Went into

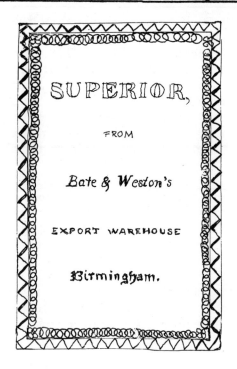

Two Birmingham labels found on the same metal tray.
Fig.652A & B

business with Buckley, a partnership that was dissolved
in 1827. Built his own tinshop and barn in 1827. Married "Maria Francis" in 1829. Went into the tin business with James A. Thompson in 1830. The firm of Goodrich and Thompson moved to Augusta, Maine in 1833. In
1835 Goodrich sold out to Charles S. Buckley, son of
Oliver. In 1837 he went back to work with Oliver, until 1842. In 1850 he joined Freeman Porter in the manufacturing of Britannia and tinware until 1852.

PATTISON (or PATERSON, or PATTERSON), EDWARD. Berlin,
Connecticut. Although Shem Drowne was one of the first
tinplate workers in America, Pattison probably influenced the growth of the industry more by introducing to
Connecticut, circa 1750, tin utensils of every description and the "flowering" of trinket boxes, etc. He was
the "father of the Yankee peddler" and when he died in
1787 his sons, Shuball and Edward, Jr. carried on the
business in their father's shop. Edward, Jr. died in
1809. In 1797 Shuball and his partner, Elisha Peck, had
a tin shop and general store, to approximately 1818.

PONTYPOOL, WALES (1670-1822). The metal (iron plate)
trays and the process of japanning them was first developed in Pontypool. The pierced edging was a distinction and the tortoiseshell background was characteristic. Fine gilt brush-stroke borders and chinoiseries in
low relief (see INDIAN WORK in the "Vocabulary") re-
flected the oriental lacquer techniques. Painted fruits
and flowers in the manner of the painters of porcelain
were also typical. The fashion, at first called "Indian," soon became known as "japanning," a name that has
survived to the present day for any painting and/or varnishing on metal plate.

Credit for the success of the Pontypool works must go to
one family, the Allgoods, five generations of them.
Little is known of the decorators. Retailers emphasized
the origin of this ware by selling it as "the real Pontypool japanned ware," with the result that "Pontypool"
soon became a generic term. Wolverhampton and Birmingham japanners, some of them from Pontypool, whose basic

japan work was in time of lesser quality (liable to
flake and crack), sold their productions as "Pontypool
japan," which has caused confusion to the present day,
especially in the case of the freehand bronzed-and-
painted double border rectangular trays, frequently miscalled "Pontypool trays."

STEVENS PLAINS. Three or four miles west of Portland,
Maine, is today called Westbrook. The land was first
cleared by Zachariah Brackett of Falmouth, Maine in
1798; his grandson, Zachariah Stevens, established the
first tinshop on the Plains, which later became a thriv-
ing craft center. The tin industry continued to grow
until, by 1832, there were 11 tinshops manufacturing
over $27,000 worth of tin annually, and sending out
over 100 tin peddlers to sell their wares in New Hampshire and Maine, and as far north as the Canadian border.
Zachariah's sons, Alfred and Samuel, took over the business in 1830 and carried it on until 1842, when the shop
was destroyed by fire. The industry declined, and by
the late 1850's, the last of the tinshops had disappear-
ed.

USK, WALES (1763-1860). A village seven miles from
Pontypool, ten miles NNE of Newport, Monmouthshire. Here
japanned ware was manufactured by members of the Allgood
family from Pontypool. Usk shapes were chiefly octagonal or "double four-S shape" (Gothic). The octagonal tray
was also a favorite with a plain center and metal leaf
work along the border and edge. Stormont (see the "Vocabulary") was used on a maroon or chocolate brown background. It is difficult to decide which pieces originated in Pontypool and which were made in Usk.

WOLVERHAMPTON. Fifteen miles NW of Birmingham, England.
It is said that japanning began in Wolverhampton between
1720 and 1750. The industry in this town had the ambi-
tion to excel in the artistic quality of its decorative
work rather than to compete with Birmingham in multi-
plying the variety of articles and uses to which papier-
mâché could be adapted. Wolverhampton remained for the
main part a tin center. The manufacturers confined

themselves largely to tea trays, many of them painted by
artists of repute, which often took on the quality of a
valuable painting and were more wall hangings than trays.
The freehand bronze and painted, double-border, rectangular tray, so often miscalled a Pontypool tray, may be
attributed to Wolverhampton. Henry Loveridge (see the
entry for LOVERIDGE, HENRY, & CO. under "Manufacturers
and Manufactories") was one of the last firms, working
in Wolverhampton until 1904. Below is a list of some of
the outstanding people and companies connected with Wolverhampton, arranged in alphabetical order.

Barney & Ryton
Bratt, J. & A.
Fearncombe, W. H.
Illridge, Henry
Mander, Benjamin
Mapplebeck & Lowe, tinware and papier-mâché suppliers
    only
Perry, Edward
Ryton, William & Obadiah
Shoolbred, Loveridge & Shooolbred (later H. Loveridge)
Taylor & Jones

MANUFACTURERS
and
MANUFACTORIES

AMERICAN TEA TRAY WORKS (1860-1878). One of the first
stamped-out trays in America was presumed to have been
done by George L. Jones in Albany, New York in 1851. In
Union Village, now Greenwich, New York, he founded what
came to be known as the American Tea Tray Works. Production started in June 1860. Two sons worked in the
factory and two daughters -- Lois and Lizzie -- decorated. Other decorators were Deborah Owen, Anna Giles,
Alta Rood, Libbie Rose, Mary Thompson, and Katie Ken-
nedy.

The japanned ware was stamped from the best imported
sheet iron and block tin. The edges of the trays, except for the very small ones, were rolled over wire.
The trays were then japanned and rubbed down. The decorating was done on black backgrounds. Each decorator
had her own pattern which consisted of leaves, usually
veined and outlined in gold leaf. Sometimes the whole
leaf was gold leaf, etched with umber or painted green,
then dusted with bronze powder. The trays were striped
in bronze. After decoration, the design only was varnished, or a substitute was applied. These oval trays
were from 6 1/2" to 30" across. Some patterns were
found in several sizes. The forerunner of this type of
tray, in England, was called a Windsor tray. The ones
made in Greenwich were aptly called Greenwich ovals.

A financial crisis hit the village in 1878. The business, mill, and stock were sold. See Fig.194 & 195.

BATEMAN & STEVENS. Salem, Connecticut. Manufacturers of
bellows. Many bellows were imported and distributed by
different companies. See Fig.328 & 329.

BLAKESLEY HALL. Birmingham, England. This is an annex
to the Birmingham Museum and Art Gallery. It houses a
rare collection of Sheldon japanned wares and patterns.
(Ebenezer Sheldon, 1827- ?). From Mr. George Goodman's
patent of transferring designs (1852) the Sheldon shop
made ample use of this form of decoration. The Sheldon
collection, beside the japanned ware, consists of hand-
drawn designs, mostly in pencil, paper templates, gold-
leaf transfers, and pin-pricked outlines. These designs

have notes and memoranda, and tell what medium was used
as well as, here and there, a worker's name. JAMES
HINKS is mentioned for some designs attributed to him.
In 1878 he was hired by the Sheldon shop on a part-time
basis. Most of the Sheldon products were papier-mâché.
See Fig.282.

CERMENATI, B. & MONFRINO. Bernard (or Barnard) Cermenati was carver, gilder, picture-framer, and looking glass
manufacturer in Newburyport, Massachusetts, Boston,
Massachusetts, and in Portsmouth, New Hampshire in the
early 1800's. Monfrino was his partner occasionally,
but mostly he worked alone. See Fig.423.

CLAY, HENRY. 1735-1812. Manufacturer and decorator.
The most important japanner in Birmingham in the clos-
ing decades of the 18th century. He served his appren-
ticeship under John Baskerville. Clay was one of the
first of the metal japanners to realize the great pos-
sibilities of the papier-mâché industry, which had been
introduced into Birmingham from France in 1755. About
1772 he took out a patent for the manufacture of boards
or panels which he called "paperware." In 1802 he re-
established in King Street, Covent Garden, London, and
became "Japanner to His Majesty King George III." Clay
died in 1812, but his associates continued under the
name of Clay & Co. until at least 1860. Many of his tea
trays and pieces are impressed on the back with the mark:
"Clay Patent," with a crown superimposed, or "Clay, King
St. Covent Garden." His descendants used the mark
"Clay, London" with the crown.

Clay's earliest mark.

Fig.653A

Various Clay marks. A crown appears over most of Clay's
later pieces (lower right).   Fig.653B-E

DOVER STAMPING COMPANY. This was founded in Boston in
1833. From its third catalog, published in 1871, we
learn that they were "Manufacturerers and Dealers in
Tinners' Hard Ware and Furnishing Goods." From old cat-
alogs we are able to date pieces and learn their correct
names. The Dover Stamping Company is still in existence,
celebrating its 136th year in business. Now located in
Fall River, Massachusetts, it continues to stamp out
utilitarian metal items such as pails, tubs, garbage
pails, trash cans and waste baskets. See Fig.80.

DREW, JOHN, of Drew & Hixon, had a shop near the Warren
Bridge in Boston in the years 1836-1850. They made
hearth bellows and imported "the fancy japanned styles."
See Fig.332.

EAST INDIA COMPANY. This was the name given to a number
of companies set up by various European countries in the
17th and 18th centuries for the purpose of engaging in
maritime trade with the East. The name usually refers
to the English East India Company founded in 1600 by
Queen Elizabeth. This company survived until 1858 and
was important because it helped to establish British
rule in India. It established large trading posts in
the East and was responsible for bringing lacquerware
for Queen Catherine's personal dowry, which was the be-
ginning of the popularity of such ware in England and

Europe. (Oriental lacquer was of great antiquity, dat-
ing back to the 12th century B.C.)

Sign of the East India Co.   Fig.654

FISHER, ROBERT. A Baltimore cabinet maker in the Sheraton style, circa 1800-1815. We identify him by his
labels on furniture. He was listed in the Baltimore di-
rectories as a cabinetmaker. He used scenic paintings
and gold-leaf borders as decorations. See Fig.564.

GARDNER, MASSACHUSETTS. Approximately in 1805 James
Comee, "father of the chair business in Gardner," began
making chairs of wood with flagg seats, entirely by hand
with only the help of a foot lathe. He employed several
young men as apprentices, some of whom later entered the
chair business for themselves. By 1878, when Herrick
wrote The History of Gardner, there were twelve chair
shops manufacturing nearly two million chairs a year.
In these 160 years, the chair and furniture business has
continued to grow in and around Gardner, and today several companies are still operating, which were in existence over a hundred years ago. Some still specialize
in early American styles. Although the once "largest
chair in the world" is no longer on display at the de-
pot, Gardner continues to be known as "The Chair City."
See the entry under HEYWOOD, LEVI, below.

GOODRICH, IVES & RUTTY CO. Nathan Goodrich of Meriden,
Connecticut, was a tinsmith who began to make plain and
japanned tinware about 1830. The name of the firm was
Goodrich and Rutty. In 1852 he was joined by Ely Ives
and Elias Howell, a painter. The firm was then called
Goodrich, Ives & Rutty Co.

HEYWOOD, LEVI. 1800-1882, manufacturer of chairs in
Gardner, Massachusetts, invented chairmaking machinery
that helped the industry of the township from 1805.
See Fig.655.

HEYWOOD WAKEFIELD COMPANY. This Gardner, Massachusetts
firm was established in 1826 when "the Heywood Brothers"
began making chairs in a small shed adjacent to their
father's farmhouse, which is where the city hall now
stands.   The business thrived, and by the time the Rev.
William D. Herrick wrote The History of Gardner in 1878,
this company was making 450,000 chairs a year.   Circa
1860 Thomas and Edward Hill came to work in the factory,
"painting chairs with landscapes and baskets of fruit
and flowers, plentifully decorated with gold leaf."
(See Fig.549.)   For several years they decorated chairs
in an assembly-line fashion, repeating one step at a
time on a group of twelve chairs.   They were true artist-
craftsmen.   Later Edward Hill settled in New Hampshire
and became well-known for his White Mountain paintings,
while Thomas Hill went to California and made a name for
himself as "the great painter of the Yosemite Valley."
This company continued to expand and today owns factories and warehouses in various parts of the country, producing a wide line of furniture.

Chairs by the Heywood Wakefield Company.   See also Fig.
548 & 549.   Fig.655

HILL, THOMAS and EDWARD.   See the preceding entry: HEY-
WOOD WAKEFIELD COMPANY.

HITCHCOCK, LAMBERT (1795-1852).   He was a native of
Cheshire, Connecticut, and in 1818 he settled in Barkhamsted, Connecticut.   Here he established a chair fac-

The Hitchcock Factory as it looked in Lambert Hitchcock's day, in Hitchcocks-ville, Connecticut, known today as Riverton. Fig.656

tory in 1825, and soon the settlement around it became known as Hitchcocks-ville.

At first he made only chair parts which he shipped as far south as Charleston, South Carolina, but he soon went over to manufacturing whole chairs, and in due course was turning out as many as 15,000 a year. His chairs were signed: "L. Hitchcock, Hitchcocks-ville Conn. Warranted."

However, since so much of his trade was on consignment, expenses running high and the money slow to come in, the business failed, and Hitchcock was declared bankrupt in 1829. In 1832 he went into business with his brother-in-law. Henceforth the signature on his chairs read: "Hitchcock, Alford & Co., Hitchcocks-ville, Conn. Warranted."

In 1849 Hitchcock left Barkhamsted and settled in Unionville, Connecticut. Here he made and sold cabinet furniture, leaving the chair business to the Hitchcocks-ville

manufactory. The Unionville business was based on the
hope that the nearby Farmington Canal would make shipping
conditions cheaper and easier, but the advent of the rail-
road made the canal obsolete, and again Hitchcock was unable to prosper.

He died in 1852, having created a chair style that bore
his name, and has meanwhile become a generic term for
all chairs of this type -- akin to the Sheraton Fancy,
beautifully decorated with stenciling, banding, and
striping, and eminently durable. The factory that bore
his name continued operations until 1840. Today it has
been restored, and the Hitchcock Chair Company of Riverton, Connecticut turns out Hitchcock chairs and furniture
of which Lambert Hitchcock could have been proud. The
Company owns rights to both signatures, and signs all its
products: "L. Hitchcock, Hitchcocks-ville Conn. Warranted," with a small distinguishing (R) at the lower right.

HULL AND STAFFORD. They manufactured tinware toys in
Clinton, Connecticut in the 1850's. Hull was a chair
stenciler.

ILLIDGE & CO. Wolverhampton, England. Did early bronze
pictures in 1818, after which they did work in gold and
pearl, as the latter came into fashion circa 1830. This
was a firm that marked some of its products. Company
dates: circa 1790-1840. See Fig.213, possibly an Illidge
piece.

INGRAHAM, ELIAS. 1805-1885. Bristol, Connecticut. Made
steeple clocks. His working years were from 1843-1848.
His firm was listed as "Brewster & Ingraham, Bristol, Ct.
U.S."

JENNENS & BETTRIDGE. Birmingham, England, 1816-1864.
The best known of all papier-mâché manufacturers. They
also japanned ironware. In 1816 they took over Henry
Clay's factory. In 1825 they took out a patent for ornamented papier-mâché with pearl shell. To this they
added gold leaf and achieved a highly striking effect.
On work tables, boxes, chairs, sofas, piano castings,

sides, lap desks, etc. the decoration was for the most part so-called "Chippendale" painting.

They employed highly skilled artists and designers and spared no expense to make their goods as nearly perfect as possible. Their name can be found impressed on the back of their papier-mâché articles. Later "Makers to the Queen" and a crown were added. In some cases the name was finely painted in, at the edge of the picture. They had showrooms in London, and for one year in New York.

Jennens & Bettridge signatures
Fig.657

LITCHFIELD MANUFACTURING COMPANY (1850-1854). Located on the Bantam River in Litchfield, Connecticut, it employed about 50 to 70 men and women for the purpose of making articles of leather, such as daguerreotype cases and their metal trimmings, also articles of wood and papier-mâché. The latter were made in the best manner from pasted-paper panels, not by the common method using pulped paper. Other pieces made in Litchfield were boxes, handscreens and clock cases bearing the company's name. English and German artists did the work and an artist from Jennens & Bettridge undoubtedly did the pearl work since they had the patent at the time (1825). The pearl shell was probably purchased ready-processed. In 1851, the company supplied the clocks as well as the cases. Perhaps due to an injudicious combining with several clock firms, the Litch-

field Manufacturing Company failed in 1855. See Fig.392.
LOVERAGE, HENRY, & CO. of Wolverhampton, England (1862-
1904/18). Makers of all kinds of tin and paper ware,
some of which was readily identifiable because of the
signature impressed on the back. They often used an
unusual treatment on the flat edge of the upturned rim
(about 3/8" wide) of black Chinese characters or calligraphy painted on gold. These trays, still existant,
are in the concave "King Gothic" and rectangular forms.
See "Shoolbred," page. 305.

McCALLUM AND HODGSON (1866-1920) took over the business from Jennens & Bettridge in Birmingham, England.
In 1887 they also took over the business of Alsager
and Neville, and in 1908 that of Perman and Stamp.
James McCallum had been trained at Jennens & Bettridge,
but was more successful as a business man than an artist when he joined Edward Hodgson, and they became
the last survivors of the industry. They manufactured
a style of pearl which had a quality of extreme neat-
ness and symmetry.

OLD HALL WORKS, THE (Turton's Hall), Wolverhampton,
England. A factory building manufacturing decorated
wares on papier-mâché and tin which was occupied in
1760 by Taylor & Jones; in 1775 by William and Obadiah
Ryton; in 1810 by William Ryton and Benjamin Walton
(Ryton & Walton); in 1842 by Benjamin Walton. They
went into bankruptcy in 1845.

B.WALTON&CO

(1842)

Fig.658

ROBINSON, CHARLES R. (circa 1805-1875), came to Rochester, N.Y. from Connecticut with his brothers in 1825.
He manufactured and decorated (or had decorated) chairs,
mostly rockers, from 1845-1860. One of his favorite
patterns was a simple one-piece stencil of two roses
and grapes. He also decorated two-slat-back chairs

with unturned legs and posts. Another one of his patterns of a small bird was also popular.

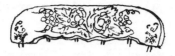

Robinson Rocker Top Slat
Fig.659

RYTON & WALTON (1810-1842), Wolverhampton, England. A
japanning firm located at the Old Hall Works. The paper trade was only a side line; japanning of metal
wares was much more important. The later bronze work
was developed in Wolverhampton and the best was done on
papier-mâché, most of it at Walton's.

SHELDON, EBENEZER, see BLAKESLEY HALL, page 296.

SHOOLBRED, WILLIAM (circa 1840-1848). The origin of
the William Shoolbred firm may be traced back to Benjamin Mander (1792) of Wolverhampton, England. With
his son Charles it became Benjamin Mander & Son. One
of their trays was an octagonal 30" x 22" with Chinese
borders in shaded gold leaf, shown below. Today trays
of this type are hard to find.

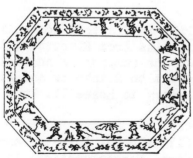

Fig.660

In 1803 Charles added the making of varnishes to the
business. About 1840, he sold the business to William
Shoolbred. In 1850 it became Shoolbred, Loveridge and
Shoolbred; then from 1862 to 1918 was listed as H.

(Henry) Loveridge & Co. Mander and his successors were
better known as japanners of metal ware, but they did
manufacture a small amount of papier-mâché.

1. Benjamin Mander (1792-1819)
2. Benjamin Mander & Son (Charles, c.1801)
3. Wm. Shoolbred (c.1840-1848)
4. Wm. Shoolbred, H. Loveridge (1848)
5. Shoolbred, Loveridge & Shoolbred (c.1850)
6. Henry Loveridge & Co. Ltd. (1862-1918)

SMALL & SON, GUEST, CHOPPING & BILL, MESSRS., Birmingham, England. By 1780 this firm had already begun to
make papier-mâché panels and, very probably, tea trays.
When Henry Clay's patent expired they, and after them,
their sons, made papier-mâché blanks and supplied them
to japanners for ornamentation. They took over Henry
Clay's business in 1802 and were succeeded by Jennens
& Bettridge in 1816.

SPIERS & SON of Oxford, England, were purchasers of
papier-mâché blanks. Some they acquired from Alsager
and Neville, partially decorated, probably by the fine
gilders the latter firm employed. Spiers & Son were
noted for their paintings of Oxford buildings and
views. Some of their articles are signed on the back.
See Fig.307.

UNION CHAIR COMPANY in Winsted, Connecticut (1849-
1882), only four miles from Riverton (Hitchcocks-ville).
From 1838 to 1840 the company belonged to Holmes &
Roberts who sold out to Hitchcock and Alford. They in
turn sold the factory to Moses II, Paul N. and Caleb
C. Camp.

WILLARD, SIMON (1753-1848), inventor and clock maker,
was born in Grafton, Massachusetts. At the age of
twelve he was apprenticed to a clock maker named Morris.
His first clocks were signed "Simon Willard, Grafton."
Circa 1780 he set up his shop in Roxbury and worked
there until he retired in 1839. He never used paintings of naval battles, landscapes, nor an American flag

on his clocks. His favorite painting was an ornamental design. He used an acorn-shaped piece (ball with
leaves) for a finial, and on his presentation pieces,
an eagle. On these pieces he also used a base. It is
believed that Simon used only brass works. There were
four Willard brothers: Benjamin, 1743-1803; Ephraim,
1755 to circa 1835; Aaron, 1757-1844; and Simon. Aaron
retired in 1823. He had a son, Aaron Jr., who took
over his father's business from 1823 to 1850. See
Fig. 406 (Simon) and Figs.396, 397 (Aaron).

BIBLIOGRAPHY

ADAMS, RUTH. Pennsylvania Dutch Art. Cleveland, World
    Publishing, 1950.

AMERICAN FEDERATION OF ARTS. Masterpieces of 101 Amer-
    ican Primitive Painters. Garden City, Doubleday,
    1962.

American Heritage. 1956-1958. American Heritage Pub-
    lishing Co., Inc., U. S. A.

Annals of Science, The. Vol. 6, no. 4; vol. 7, no. 1,
    2, 4; vol. 9, no. 1, 3.

Antiques Magazine. 1922-1968.

ARONSON, JOSEPH. The Encyclopedia of Furniture. New
    York, Crown, 1935.

Art Journal, The. Formerly The Art Union. 1849, 1851-
    1858, 1862, 1863, 1866, 1867.

Art Union, The. 1845-1848.

AVERY, AMOS G. New England Clocks at Sturbridge Vil-
    lage. Meriden, Meriden Gravure, 1955.

BRAZER, ESTHER STEVENS. "Butler Tinware." Antiques,
    August 1945.

------. Early American Decoration. Springfield, Pond-
    Ekberg, 1940.

CARLISLE, LILIAN BAKER. Hatboxes and Bandboxes at the
    Shelburne Museum. Shelburne, Shelburne Museum, 1960.

CESCINSKY, HERBERT. English Furniture from Gothic to
    Sheraton. New York, Garden City Publishing, 1937.
    Dover Publications, 1968.

Chronicle of the Museum for the Arts of Decorations of
    the Cooper Union. New York, John B. Watkins, 1951.

CLARK, ARTHUR. The Story of Pontypool. Wales, Ponty-
    pool Urban District Council to Commemorate the Fes-
    tival of Wales, 1958.

COFFIN, MARGARET MATTISON. American Country Tinware,
    1700-1900. Camden, New Jersey, Thomas Nelson &
    Sons, 1968.

------. "Dictionary of American Painted Furniture."
    Woman's Day, July 1966.

------. "Dictionary of American Painted Tinware."
    Woman's Day, July 1964.

COLE, ANN TILBORN. How to Identify Antiques. New York,
    McKay, 1957.

COMSTOCK, HELEN. American Furniture. New York, Viking
    Press, 1962.

------. The Looking-Glass in America, 1700-1825. New
    York, Viking Press, 1968.

Connecticut Historical Society. Vol. 23, no.1, Jan-
    uary 1958; vol. 25, no. 3, July 1960; vol. 34,
    no.1, January 1969. Hartford.

"Decorative Metalware." House Beautiful, September
    1914.

Decorators. Publication of the Historical Society of
    Early American Decoration, Inc.

DeVOE, SHIRLEY SPAULDING. American Decorated Chairs.
    New Milford, Mock and Marsh, 1947.

------. "Clay's Paper Trays." Antiques, February 1956.

------. "The Decline of Japanning." Antiques, Decem-
    ber 1954.

------. Tinsmiths of Connecticut. Middleton, Wesleyan
    University Press, 1968.

DICKINSON, GEORGE. English Papier-Mâché. London,
    Courier Press, 1925.

DOERNER, MAX. Materials of the Artist and Their Use
    in Painting. New York, Harcourt Brace, 1949.

DOLAN, J. R. The Yankee Peddlers of Early America.
    New York, Bramhall House, 1964.

DOVER STAMPING CO. Catalogue. Third issue. New Bed-
    ford, 1871.

DREPPERD, CARL. American Clocks and Clockmakers.
    Boston, Branford.

------. Pioneer America, Its First Three Centuries. Garden City, Doubleday, 1949.

------. The Primer of American Antiques. Garden City, Doubleday, 1944.

Encyclopaedia Britannica. 11th edition, 1911. London, Cambridge University Press.

FENN, ARMOR. Design and Tradition. Great Britain, 1920.

"Field of Art, The." Scribner's, October 1915.

FILLEY, OLIVER. The Oliver Filley Papers. Hartford, Connecticut State Library.

FORBES, ESTHER. Rainbow on the Road. Boston, Houghton Mifflin, 1954.

FRERE-COOK, GERVIS. The Decorative Arts of the Mariner. Boston, Little Brown, 1966.

Funk and Wagnall Dictionary and Encyclopedia. 1946, 1951.

"Furniture Makers and Decorators of the XVII and XVIII Centuries." The Curio, vol. 1, no. 4, December 1887.

GOULD, MARY EARLE. Antique Tin and Tole Ware. Rutland, Charles E. Tuttle, 1958.

GROSS, LESLIE. Housewife's Guide to Antiques.

Guide to the Collections of Pontypool and Usk Japan. Wales, National Museum of Wales and the Press Board of the University of Wales, 1926.

HALLETT, CHARLES. Furniture Decorating Made Easy. Boston, Charles T. Branford, 1952.

HANSON, H. J. European Folk Art. New York, McGraw-Hill Book Co., 1968.

HONOUR, HUGH. Chinoiserie. London, John Murray, 1961.

HUGHES, BERNARD and THERLE. Small Antique Furniture. New York, Macmillan, 1958.

HUGHES, G. BERNARD. "Skill of the Pontypool Japanners." Country Life Annual, 1968.

JOHN, WILLIAM D. Pontypool and Usk Japanned Wares.
    Newport, Monmouthshire, England, Ceramic Book Co.,
    1953.

------. English Decorated Trays. Newport, Monmouth-
    shire, England, Ceramic Book Co., 1964.

KAUFFMAN, HENRY. Pennsylvania Dutch American Folk Art.
    New York, Dover Publications, 1964.

KOIZUMI, GUNJI. Lacquer Work. London, Putnam and
    Sons, 1923.

KOVAL, RALPH and TERRY. American Country Furniture,
    1780-1875. New York, Crown, 1965.

LEA, ZILLA. Ornamented Chair. A publication of the
    Historical Society for Early American Decoration.
    Rutland, Charles Tuttle, 1960.

LICHTEN, FRANCES. Folk Art of Rural Pennsylvania.
    New York, Scribner, 1946.

LIPMAN, JEAN. American Folk Decoration. New York, Ox-
    ford University Press, 1951.

------. American Primitive Painting. New York, Oxford
    University Press, 1942.

------. Rufus Porter, Yankee Pioneer. New York,
    Clarkson N. Potter, Inc., 1968.

LITTLE, NINA FLETCHER. American Decorative Wall Paint-
    ing, 1700-1850. New York, Old Sturbridge Village in
    cooperation with Studio Publications, 1952.

------. Country Art in New England, 1790-1840. Meriden,
    Meriden Gravure Co., 1960.

LORD, P.S., & FOLEY, D. J. Folk Arts and Crafts of New
    England. Philadelphia, Chilton, 1965.

MAYER, RALPH. Artist's Handbook of Materials and Tech-
    niques. New York, Viking Press, 1948.

McCLINTON, KATHERINE MORRISON. Handbook of Popular
    Antiques. New York, Random House, 1946.

------. American Country Antiques. Coward-McCann,
    Inc., 1967.

MILLER, EDGAR G. Jr. American Antique Furniture. 2 volumes. New York, Barrows and Co., 1937.

MONTGOMERY, CHARLES R. American Furniture -- The Federal Period. New York, Viking, 1966.

MOORE, MABEL ROBERTS. Hitchcock Chairs. New Haven, Yale University Press, 1933.

Museum and Garden Guide for Winterthur. Knebels Press, 1956.

NATIONAL GALLERY OF ART. 101 American Primitive Water Colors and Pastels. Washington, Garbisch Collection.

NUTTING, WALLACE. Clock Book. Garden City, Garden City Publishing, 1935.

------. Furniture Treasury. 2 volumes. New York, Macmillan, 1908.

ORMSBEE, THOMAS H. Field Guide to Early American Furniture. Boston, Little, Brown, 1951. New York, Bantam.

------. Know Your Heirlooms. New York, McBride, 1957.

------. Antique Digest.

Oxford Encyclopedia.

PALMER, BROOKS. The Book of American Clocks. New York, Macmillan, 1950.

------. The Romance of Time. New Haven, Connecticut, 1954.

PERROTT, A. "Notable Collection of Tole." House Beautiful, February 1924.

POST, ELLWOOD. Saints, Signs and Symbols. London, Morehouse-Barlow, 1962.

POWERS, BEATRICE FARNSWORTH and FLOYD, OLIVE. Early American Decorated Tin. New York, Hastings House, 1957.

ROBACKER, EARL F. Pennsylvania Dutch Stuff. Philadelphia, University of Pennsylvania Press, 1944.

ROTH, RODRIS. Floor Coverings in 18th Century America.

Washington, D. C., U. S. Government Printing Office, 1967.

SABINE, ELLEN S. Early American Decorative Patterns. New York, D. Van Nostrand, 1962.

SACK, ALBERT. Fine Points of Furniture. New York, Crown Publishing, 1950.

SAYER, ROBERT. The Ladies Amusement or The Whole Art of Japanning Made Easy. London, Facsimile edition, 1959.

SCOTT, VIOLET. Art in America, page 52 of the Spring-Summer 1957 issue.

SELDON, MARJORIE WARD. The Interior Paint of the Campbell-Whittlessey House, 1835-1836. Rochester, Society for the Preservation of Landmarks in Western New York, 1949.

SHOEMAKER, ALFRED L. Hex, No! Pennsylvania, The Pennsylvania Dutch Folklore Center, Inc., 1953.

STALKER, JOHN and PARKER, GEORGE. A Treatise of Japanning, Varnishing and Guilding. London, Portland Press Ltd., 1960.

STEPHENSON, JESSIE BANE. From Old Stencils to Silk Screening. New York, Charles Scribner's Sons, 1953.

SZE, MAI-MAI. The Chinese Way of Painting. New York, Random House, 1956.

THOMAS, GERTRUDE Z. Richer Than Spices. New York, Alfred A. Knopf, 1961.

THOMAS, T. H. Pontypool Japan Ware. Cardiff, 1906.

TOILER, JANE. Papier-Mâché in Great Britain and America. London, G. Bell and Sons Ltd., 1962.

UKHANOVA, I.N. Russian Lacquer in the Hermitage, Leningrad.

WARING, JANET. Early American Stencil Decorations. Watkins Glen, Century House, reissue of 1937.

------. Early American Wall Stencils. New York, Wm. R. Scott, Inc., 1937.

Waterways Museum, The. London, British Waterways Board,
    1964.

Webster's Dictionary. Springfield. C. G. Merriam, 1909.

WILLARD, JOHN WARE. Simon Willard and His Clocks. New
    York, Dover, 1968. First edition was published in
    1911.

WINCHESTER, ALICE W. The Antiques Book. New York, A.
    Wyn, Inc., 1950.

------. How to Know American Antiques. New York, New
    American Library of World Literature, Inc., 1951.

------. Living with Antiques. New York, Dutton, 1963.

WRIGHT, FLORENCE E. How to Stencil Chairs. New York,
    Privately published, 1949.

------. Three Centuries of Furniture. Ithaca, Cornell
    Extension Bulletin, 1950.

VOCABULARY

ACANTHUS. A conventionalized leaf
used as a decorative motif in ornamentation and furniture design.
Greek and Roman origins.

ACORN. Used in design and ornamentation of furniture, clocks and tinware. Sometimes as finial or pendant.

ADAM STYLE. Furniture as developed by the Adam brothers: John, Robert — the most famous (1728-1792), James,
and William (1730-1794). The brothers practiced as
architects while employing cabinet makers and painters
to carry out their designs. There was a transition
period between mahogany (1720-1765) and satinwood
(1765-1800). It was on the latter that they featured
much painted decoration, exquisitely done. Gilding
over a base of white or green paint was extensively
employed. In America their influence made itself felt
chiefly in looking glasses and mantel pieces. The
fashion lasted for about twenty-five years (1765-1790).
The Adam style is often called "neo-classic "

ALIZARIN CRIMSON. A transparent paint used over stenciling, etc. A deep clear red.

ALUMINUM LEAF. A book of 5½" square sheets. Used for
lettering and decorative art work.

ANGEL WING. A rail on some rockers
and chairs in the shape of "angel
wings."

ANTHEMION. The honeysuckle or palm leaf pattern in
decorative design. Common in Greek architectural decoration. Popularized by the Adam brothers.

ANTHEMION. Description
on preceding page.

ANTIQUE. Belonging to a former era. One hundred years
ago or older (legal definition). Before 1830 (the be-
ginning of the machine age) for antiquarians.

ANTIQUING. Treating wood or finish on furniture, etc.
to make it look old.

APRON. The structural part beneath
a chair seat. Also called skirt or
banded seat. The cabinet work term
is "valence."

ARABESQUE. A flat ornamentation employing interlaced
lines and curves, as in Arabian architecture. Pertaining to fanciful ornamentation. Brown scrolls with gold
leaf accents.

ARCHITECTURAL. An ordered arrangement of the parts of
an object. Properly designed. Pertaining to buildings
and their design.

ARCHITECTURAL CLOCK. A combination of columns and pillars used in the construction of a clock.

ARCHITECTURAL LOOKING GLASS. A combination of columns
and pillars used in the construction of a looking
glass.

ARCHITECTURAL SCENE. Ink line drawings of buildings
used as decoration on clock and looking glass tablets.

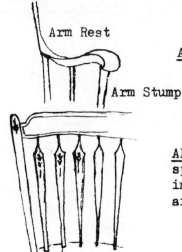

Arm Rest

Arm Stump

ARM REST and ARM STUMP.

ARROW-BACK SPINDLES. Refers to the spindles of Windsor type chairs hav- ing flattened sections formed like arrows or arrow points.

ASPHALTUM. A refined form of asphalt. A solution of mineral asphalt in varnish. Generally applied over bright tin in varying tones of brown.

AUTHENTIC. Of undisputed origin; genuine.

BACKBOARD. The thin board on the back of a looking glass to hold the glass in place. On an English look- ing glass it fits into the groove of the frame. On an American looking glass the backboard overlaps the back of the frame slightly and is tacked onto it.

BACK PAINTING, or BEHIND COLORING. The painting applied behind prints or engravings after the latter have been transferred onto glass. The base or undercoats of a painted flower or any other design.

BALL FEET. See FEET.

BALLOON BACK. A chair-back style shaped like the outline of a partial- ly inflated balloon. Developed by Hepplewhite and found mainly in Penn- sylvania.

BALLS. Pendants on architectural looking glasses. A
small sized ball usually denotes an earlier date, circa
1790. They increased in size circa 1800. Occasionally referred to as "Nelson's cannon balls." Also found
on Sheraton type and Sheraton Fancy chairs.

BALTIMORE FURNITURE. Baltimore and other parts of Maryland produced some of the finest American cabinet furniture of the eighteenth century. Queen Anne, Chippendale, Hepplewhite and Sheraton styles were important
contributions to American furniture making. The Baltimore painted furniture illustrated in this glossary is
in the Sheraton tradition and is of the late eighteenth
and early nineteenth century. It is distinguished by
the beauty of its ornamentation, rare refinement and
grace.

BALUSTER. A small column -- turned,
square or flat -- supporting a rail,
or used as architectural detail in
clocks, looking glasses and chairs.
In England the word "baluster" was
corrupted to "banister," unfortunately now in general use.

BAMBOO TURNED. A furniture part done
with ringings that resemble joints in
bamboo. Also found on cornice boards
in half rounds.

BANANA TOP. Incorrect name for bolster top.

BAND. A wide stripe on furniture, trays, etc.

BANDED SEAT. See APRON.

BANISTER. See BALUSTER.

BANJO CLOCK. Nineteenth century American wall clock in
the form of a banjo.

BARGEE ART (roses and castles). English decoration on
tin and wood, done by water gypsies who lived on canals.

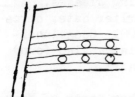

BARS. Three bars with gilded balls, found on Sheraton style chairs.

BASE PIECE. The lowest member of a piece of furniture or of a column. Also found on the bottom of some clocks.

BASIN STAND. In America called a "wash stand." In eighteenth century England spelled bason-stand.

BEADING. An applied decorative molding which looks like a series of round beads.

BEDIZENED. Adorned or dressed in a showy, gaudy manner.

BELL FLOWER. Found on Sheraton-influenced furniture, circa 1815.

BENCH. A long seat, usually without a back. In England it refers to a seat with a back, or a settee.

BERLIN WARE. Tin ware, both country painted and stenciled, made in Berlin, Connecticut from 1740-1850.

BEZEL. A groove and flange made to receive a beveled edge, such as a brass bezel to hold the glass of a clock.

BILSTON BLANK. Tinware made in Bilston, England, and sent to other shops to be decorated.

BIN. A receptacle for any commodity. See CANISTER.

BLANKET CHEST. Any chest for blanket storage, usually

with a hinged top section and a drawer in or near the base. Seventeenth and eighteenth centuries.

BLICKY, or BLICKIE. Any small tin vessel. "Blick" in Dutch means tin.

BLOCK TIN. An impure commercial tin cast in blocks.

BLOCK TINWARE. Table and cooking ware of block tin. Next to silver plate in value. Rare. Advertised in American papers 1790-1830.

BLOTTER SIDES. See SIDES.

BOAT SHAPE. Shaped like a boat or gondola.

BOB. A piece of leather, chamois or velvet, run through a hollow quill or applied to the end of a stick or Q-tip, and used to apply bronze powder to a design.

BOLECTION. A molding following the outside edge of a panel and projecting beyond the face of the frame in which the panel is held. Generally with outward roll and ogee shape in the section.

BOLSTER TOP. A chair, similar to a pillow top but with a longer "pillow." Also called "roll-top." Mis-called banana and sausage top.

BORDER. The part of the surface which is just within the boundary line or rim of a tray or object.

Fine "Hepplewhite" border

Wm. Jackson border (gold leaf)

Typical Usk borders, 1760-1860's

Pierced-edge borders
Pontypool, Wales, late 18th century

Three oval gallery tray borders

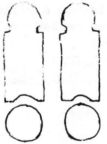

From a brazier

Keyhole piercing

BORDERER. One who paints borders.

BOSTON PATTERN. The name of a pattern, for purposes of identification, at the Dover Stamping Co.

BOTTLE STAND. See COASTER.

BOSTON ROCKER. A painted or stencil decorated rocking
chair with spindle back and roll-curved seat. Popular
1840-1860. Probably originated in Boston.

BRACKET FEET. See FEET.

BRIDE'S BOX. Pennsylvania box for the bride in which
she kept her trinkets, etc.

BRIDE'S TRAY. A name introduced by Mrs. Brazer because
the first ones she happened to find had white backgrounds. They have fine tracery and delicate painting,
usually on the flange down onto the floor. Most of the
work in gold leaf, some bronzing and fine painted detail.

BRITANNIA METAL. An alloy containing between 80 and
90% tin, with varying proportions of antimony and copper. First manufactured in Sheffield, England, by Hancock & Jessop in 1770. Britannia metal articles were
first made by stamping with dies. Then the curious
process of metal spinning was introduced: a thin sheet
of Britannia metal was placed on a wooden model of the
piece to be made; this was made to rotate on a lathe,
and steel, hardwood, bloodstone and other tools were
used to press the yielding metal into the model's shape.
Used mainly for hot-water jugs, coffee pots, sugar
bowls, soup tureens, waiters, trays, etc. Manufactured
chiefly in Sheffield and Birmingham, England, and in
Connecticut in the United States.

BRITANNIA WARE. Articles made of Britannia metal.

BRONZE POWDERS. Any fine powdered alloys or ores such
as brass, copper or tin, used in decorating.

BRONZING. The art of applying bronze powders to a
tacky surface. See FREEHAND BRONZING in the chapter
on Design.

BRUSH STROKES. Strokes done with a paint brush; used in the painted designs applied to American tinware; a part of the technique called "country painting." See COUNTRY PAINTING in the chapter on Design.

BRUNSWICK BLACK (japan). A hard asphaltum black varnish for coating sheet metal. Formula: 5 lbs. asphaltum, melted, mixed with 2 lbs. of boiled oil and 1 gal. spirits of turpentine.

BUHL (Boulle). French cabinet maker, 1642-1732. Metal or tortoise-shell inlay in furniture. Also cabinet work so decorated.

BUN BASKET. An oval or boat-shaped open tin vessel to hold buns, biscuits, etc.

BUTTON-BACK. The back slat of certain Hitchcock chairs, named for the four "buttons" that hold the slat to the stiles.

Button-back slat

CABRIOLE LEGS. See LEGS.

CADDY. A small box for keeping tea. A canister.

CALLIGRAPHY. Beautiful penmanship. Chinese characters.

CANDLE BOX. A box with a sliding cover to store candles. Keeps the mice away!

CANDLE HOLDER. A short support for candle or candles, usually with a saucer-like base.

CANDLE SHEARS or SHERES. Scissors-shaped device to trim the candlewick.

CANDLESTICK. A tall support for candles.

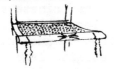

CANE SEAT. Flexible rattan, woven in open patterns for chair seats and backs.

CANISTER. A tin receptacle with a cover.

CANTERBURY. An ornamental stand for holding music or periodicals.

CARD TRAY. A small tray on which calling cards were left. Some had swinging handles.

CARTOUCHE. An ornamental emblem inlaid, painted, carved or stenciled in the shape of a heart, oval, star, etc.

CASKET. A small chest or box with a hinged lid.

CAVETTO. Concave molding.

CHEESE CRADLE. A cradle-shaped container to hold cheese.

CHESTNUT URN. A graceful, curved, funnel-shaped urn in which to store chestnuts.

CHIAROSCURO. The distribution of light and shade in a painting.

CHIMNEY BOARD. See the entry, "Fireboard."

CHIMNEY FURNITURE. Decorative accessories placed on a mantel or used with fireplaces.

CHINOISERIE. European decoration, influenced or inspired by oriental art, particularly the Chinese.

CHIPPENDALE. English furniture style named after Thomas Chippendale (1718-1799), English cabinet maker during England's most splendid period. At first he worked in the Adam style. In 1754 he published "The Gentleman and Cabinet Maker's Directory," with 160 engraved plates.

In 1759 there was a second edition and in 1762 a third.
His style was in turn akin to Louis XV, the Chinese and
the Gothic. He introduced the cabriole leg, which originated in Holland; the claw and ball foot of ancient
oriental origin; the straight, square Georgian leg;
the carved latticework Chinese leg; the Gothic fretwork leg; the rococo leg with curled or hoofed foot.
A Gothic feeling is evident in his chair backs which
often took the form of a church or oval rose window.

CHIPPENDALE PAINTING. A style of decorative painting
found on Gothic trays and other articles, probably a
term originating with Mrs. Brazer. It has nothing to
do with Thomas Chippendale or Chippendale furniture.
See the "Chippendale Painting" entry in the chapter on
"Design."

CLASSIC. Highest rank or class in art; Classical:
high standard.

CLAW FEET. See the entry, "Feet."

CLAY WARE. Invented by Henry Clay. A specially com-
pounded early type of papier-mache. See the entry,
HENRY CLAY in the chapter on "Manufacturers and Manufactories."

COAL VASE. A decorative covered receptacle for coal;
in French, "purdonium."

COASTER. A holder for a bottle or decanter which is
passed around the table, often called a "bottle stand."

COFFEE POT. A covered vessel in which coffee is prepared and served.

COFFIN or COFFIN LID TRAY. A decorated octagonal tray
under 13 3/4" long, with a narrow rim.

COLUMN. A vertical shaft or pillar, usually having a
base and a capital.

COMB-BACK. A Windsor chair with a back surmounted by a comb piece consisting of a shaped crest rail supported by spindles.

COMMODE. A piece of furniture made specifically to hold chamber ware, usually with a hinged lid.

COMMON YELLOW CHAIR. A thumb-back chair.

COMPO. Term derived from the word "composition," used for molding ornaments, repairing breaks in frames, etc. Made of boiled linseed oil, rosin, hot thick glue, and whiting, kneaded and pressed in a mold while still hot.

COMPOTE. A pedestal type dish from which fruit is served.

CONCAVE. Curved in. Opposite of convex.

CONE. A solid figure that tapers uniformly from a circular base to a point.

CONE TOP. Having a conical shape.

CONVEX. Curved out, rising into spherical or rounded form.

CORBEL. A piece serving as a cushion for a capital, as in a column.

CORK. A tool for stenciling; a stamp.

CORNICE BOARD. A frame, decorated or stenciled, which covers the rods and hooks used for draperies or Venetian blinds.

CORNUCOPIA SLAT-BACK. A horn of plenty, symbolizing peace and prosperity, found on Hitchcock chairs of the period.

COROMANDEL LACQUER. A type of Chinese lacquerwork in which the design is cut in intaglio (incised carving or sunken design) and completed with various colors and gold. Coromandel was so called because objects thus decorated were imported into western Europe by East India merchants with headquarters on the Coromandel Coast, on the eastern seaboard of India. "Mandel" means "region."

COUNTER TRAY. A tray for counters, used in the home to keep score or accounts of a game.

COUNTRY PAINTING. A style of brush stroke painting as found on American tin of the 18th century. See the entry, "Country painting" in the chapter on "Design."

COUNTRY TIN. Various articles manufactured by the country tinsmiths. First made by the New England smiths on imported tin sheets. Decorated with country painting.

COURTING MIRROR. A small wood-framed looking glass, usually a courting gift.

CREST RAIL. The top rail of a chair, sometimes painted or carved.

CRESTING. The top rail of a chair.

CRIMPED EDGE. See the entry, "Fluting," page 338.

CROOKED SPOUT. A bent spout such as that on a coffee pot.

CROSS-HATCH. A series of lines paralleling each other in both directions. Similar to lattice work.

CROWN-TOP. A crest rail with a raised center section. Found on Hitchcock chairs and rockers.

Crown-top rocker, circa 1835

Crown-top Hitchcock

Crown-top side chair

CRUMBER. A table brush for removing crumbs.

CRYSTAL PAINTING. Reverse painting on glass enriched with tin foil shining through transparent paints, giving a glittering and vivid effect. Tinsel painting.

CRYSTALLIZED TIN. New tin with a chemical applied,
giving it a crystallized appearance.

CUSHIONED FRIEZE. The rounded top drawer on an Empire
bureau.

CUT-CORNER TRAY. A tray usually with a 1" or 1 1/2"
flange. A cut-corner tray with less than a 1" flange
is a coffin or coffin-lid tray.

CUT-OUT SLAT. Used on Hitchcock-
style chairs.

CUTTING UP. A trade expression for painting or etching fine line details on gilded motifs, such as veining petal forms and flower centers. Etching or scratching in, as in fine line drawing.

CYMA CURVE. A continuous curve, one-half of which is
concave, the other convex. Used this way they formed
the outline on the skirts of highboys, etc. Also on
moldings, cupboard openings, the inner edges of mirrors
and the edges of Gothic trays.

Cyma curves found on chair backs.

This one formed the cabriole leg.

These two cyma curves placed this way form
the scroll-top on highboys, etc.

DAGUERREOTYPE. First photographic pictures made. A
thin plate of polished copper was coated with pure silver and made sensitive to light by being treated with
iodine and bromide vapors. The plate was then placed
in a camera, exposed to light and developed by vapor

of mercury and a bath of hyposulfite of soda. Prints
were not made from the plate; the plate was the picture itself, and extra pictures could be made only by
taking the picture again.

DECALCOMANIE. The art of transferring pictures to china, wood, glass,
tin, etc. The designs are printed
in color on paper, in reverse. By
dampening the back of the paper they
may be removed and adhered to the
article as desired. The effect frequently resembles painting to such
an extent that it is hard to tell
the two processes apart.

DEED BOX. See the entry for "Tin trunk."

DEUTSCH. German. Corrupted in the United States to
"Dutch," as in Pennsylvania Dutch.

DIAL. A circular plate or face as on a clock; a device for indicating time, sometimes seen with an arch.

DIAMOND SLAT-BACK. Used on Hitch-
cock-type chairs.

DIAPER PATTERN. A lattice-like decoration that has a design in each
square.

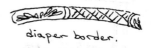

diaper border.

DIRECTOIRE (DIRECTORY). A style of furniture in France
between 1795 and 1799.

DISHED. Convexed.

DISTELFINK. A Pennsylvania German term for a stylized bird design, usually in vivid colors.

DOCUMENT BOX. See the entry for "Tin trunk."

DOOR PLATE. A decorative small tin, papier-mâché or porcelain plate affixed to a swinging door. Also called a "Finger plate."

DOUTER. A cone-shaped implement for extinguishing a candle.

DOWRY CHEST. A chest which contained the property a woman brought to her husband in marriage; a hope chest. "Dower" means: the real estate of a deceased husband which the law gives to his widow during her lifetime.

DRAGON'S BLOOD. Any of several resinous products, mostly dark red, which are used for coloring varnish.

DUODECIMAL. Pertaining to 12; 1/12.

DUTCH METAL. Five and one-half inch square sheets of metal leaf produced by subjecting thin copper to zinc fumes. The result is similar to deep gold, but it darkens and discolors rapidly. Heavier than gold leaf. Can be picked up with one's fingers.

DUTCH PINK. Yellow paint.

EAGLE SLAT-BACK. A Hitchcock-style chair with eagle-shaped slat in the middle.

EARED-BACK CHAIR. See the entry, "Thumb-back."

EBONIZE. The border or sections of borders on a glass
were sometimes painted a deep shiny black to resemble
ebony. This was also done on the turnings of non-architectural looking glasses, either all or in part.

EDGE. The extreme border or rim.

EDWARDIAN. Relating to the reign of Edward VII of England, 1841-1910.

EGG CODDLER. A container in which eggs were cooked
(coddled).

ÉGLOMISÉ. A design applied to the reverse side of glass
panels or tablets in gold or silver leaf and subsequently
engraved and backed with asphaltum. The remaining glass
is painted with opaque pigment, often water color. A
method practiced in the Middle Ages. It was named after
the Frenchman Jean Baptiste Glomi, who revived an old
technique. He died in 1786. "Verre (glass) églomisé"
was used on looking glass tablets and on furniture. Two
examples are shown below.

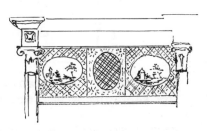

Églomisé panel or tablet: glass
decorated on the back with engraved gold and silver foils;
background, off white.

A fine églomisé tab-
let by an artist of
ability. Circa 1812.
All gold leaf, fine-
ly etched and backed
with asphaltum, then
white paint beyond
the gold leaf.

ELBOW. The joint between the back and the seat of a chair.

EMBOSS. To raise, from the surface, a design in relief.

EMBOSSING. The art of producing raised or projecting figures or designs in relief, on a surface.

EMPIRE. Refers to a French furniture style (1804-1870). Approximate dates in America: 1805-1840.

ENAMEL. A varnish with a paint pigment, an opaque, semi-transparent, or colored substance.

ENAMELING. Painting or decorating in enamel.

ENGRAVING. Ornamenting on gold, silver and other metals by incising the design with a sharp tool.

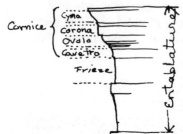

ENTABLATURE. A post and lintel construction. The part immediately above the column; frieze; central space; or the upper projecting moldings.

ESCAPEMENT. A mechanical device used in timepieces for securing a uniform movement. Found on dials.

ETCH. To outline or sketch by scratching lines with a pointed instrument.

EXTINGUISHER. A cone-shaped implement for putting out a candle.

FAN BACK. A characteristic of a Windsor chair, or the chair itself.

FANCY CHAIR. A brightly-painted or stenciled, lightweight chair, often with a rush or a cane seat, having base coats of many colors, including black. The design was sometimes in gold leaf.

FEET

Ball feet   Bracket feet   Splayed
                                    bracket foot

Claw foot   Hepplewhite spade foot   Snake foot

FEDERAL PERIOD. A period in American furniture production that includes Duncan Phyfe furniture. 1760-1840.

FIDDLE-BACK. A chair with a single
splat resembling a fiddle. Miscalled
urn, vase or banister back.

FILLET. A thin band, a strip, or an engraved line.

FILLETING. Banding or striping.

FILIGREE. A delicate ornament; all work of an intertwined nature.

FINGER PLATE. See the entry, "Door plate."

FINIAL. A decorative object at the top of the back uprights of a chair or at the corners and center of a
pediment. Usually a turned or carved piece.

FIREBOARD or CHIMNEY BOARD. A board which fits into a
fireplace opening, often covered with fancy paper, a
painted scene or a stenciled design.

FIRE BUCKET. Made of leather and often decorated with the owner's name or the insignia of a volunteer fire company.

FIRE SCREEN. A panel on a pole, adjustable to any height, to ward off the direct heat of the fire. Sometimes called a "pole screen."

FLAGG SEAT. A seat woven of rushes or flaggs.

FLANGE. The raised or projecting rim of a tray.

FLATBACK CANDLE HOLDER. An ornamental wall bracket which holds a candle. A sconce. Word used until circa 1815.

FLOOR. The main flat surface of a tray.

FLOOR CLOTH. A floor covering made of sail cloth, often painted with a Spanish tile design, geometrics, or imitation marble, in the early 1700's. Later they became floral, and in 1828, in Boston, were advertised as "painted floor cloths, without seams, some with imitation of Brussel carpeting."

FLOWER PAINTING. Neither so-called Chippendale nor lace edge painting; neither realistic nor stylized but closer to a peasant type of painting.

FLOWERED FURNITURE. Lacquered furniture of the William and Mary and Queen Anne periods, embellished with gilded flowers and scenes in the Chinese style.

FLOWERING. The art of flower decoration, painted by hand on a japanned base, such as the so-called Chippendale and lace edge painting.

FLUTING. A series of grooves, separated by a narrow fillet. The fluting or crimping machine was invented in 1815.

FOIL. See the entry, "Metal leaf."

FOOT RAIL. Front stretcher of a chair.

FOOT WARMER. A perforated box to hold a hot brick or coals with which to warm one's feet.

FORMULAS. Stencils, theorems, or poonahs.

FRAKTUR or FRAKTUR-SCHRIFTEN. A Pennsylvania German term for illuminated writings done in color with pen and brush. Widely used for various documents such as baptismal and birth certificates, certificates of merit, hymnals, house blessings and book plates. Some are done entirely in ink with no coloring. Frakturs were done in other states beside Pennsylvania.

Fraktur by Heinrich Otto, 1792
Lancaster County, Pennsylvania

Fraktur (book plate) of the Mennonite school, one of the three major schools. Schwenkfeldian and Ephrata were the other two. Dated 1797.

FRAME. An open wooden case supporting a looking glass or picture.

FREEHAND BRONZING. A method of decorating favored in the 18th and 19th centuries in which bronze powders were applied freehand to a tacky varnish base. See the entry for "Freehand bronzing" in the chapter on "Design."

FRESCO. A painting done on freshly spread plaster before it dries.

FRETWORK. Scrolled openwork, varying in intricacy, in crests and aprons of looking glasses and on furniture.

FRONT-ROLL SEAT.

FROSTED. A cloudy surface produced on glass, in imitation of frost.

GADROON or GODROON. A pattern of repeated curved and fluted elements used on moldings or edges of furniture.

GALLERY. A small railing or raised
straight rim, frequently pierced.

GENRE PAINTING.   A style of painting depicting scenes
of everyday life.

GEORGIAN PERIOD.   1714-1830.

GESSO. Plaster made of whiting and glue, used for
raised decorations, etc.

GILD. To coat with gold or metal leaf or a gold-color-
ed substance.

GILDER'S GLASS. Tablets for looking glasses, coarsely
and heavily etched by the craftsman who built and gilded the looking glass, rather than by an artist who
specialized in such delicate and elegant work. Gilder's
glass bears a crude similarity to églomise. Two examples are shown below.

Gold leaf design on
the back of the
glass, backed with
paint. Circa 1820.

GILDING. The application of various types of gold or
metal leaf to tin, glass and other surfaces.

GILT. Gilded, gold in color, golden. The gold or whatever material applied in gilding. Refers to the less

refined work.   See also the entry for "Gold leaf," below.

GIRANDOLE.   A bracket for candles or a branched candlestick.   A mirror with candle holders.

GIRANDOLE MIRROR (1800).   A large convex mirror, introduced from France in the late 18th century.   It was
usually circular in shape and enclosed in a cavetto
frame, studded with gilt balls.   It had girandoles and
was often surmounted by an eagle.   Used usually for decorative purposes, the girandole mirror reflects an entire room in perspective.   This term now seems to apply
to all convex mirrors whether they have candle arms or
not.

GLASS PAPER.   Ground glass glued to paper.   Used for
striking matches.

GLAZING.   A painted thin wash coat over parts of the
design to subdue the base color, usually transparent
overlaying with something shiny.

GOLD LEAF.   Twenty-three carat gold, beaten to thin
sheets.   Alloying with silver or copper alters the pur
rity and color.   Term used for the finest work of this
type.   See the entry for "Gilt," above.

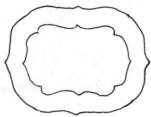

GOTHIC.   The point-and-curve style
in architecture and tray shapes. In
the case of trays, miscalled "Chippendale."   Shown here is a Gothic-
shape tray.

GRAINING.   Imitation of wood by various methods and on
various articles.   The types are: mahogany, putty,
rosewood, two-toned, sponge, stippled.   See the entry
on "Graining" in the chapter on "Design."

GRECIAN STYLE.   A gracious style with sweeping lines
and curves.   Frequent use of gilding to resemble bronze.

GREEK KEY or FRET. A repeated pattern of square hooked shapes as a band decoration. Favored by the Adam brothers.

GRISAILLE. Painting in shades of grey (Fr. gris) to make the work look three dimensional. Became popular in Europe in the late 17th century and was intended to simulate figures in relief.

GUINEA HOLES. The scooped-out corners in 18th century English card tables as receptacles for coins.

H-STRETCHER. Found on some Adam and Windsor chairs.

HALF-SHEET WAITER. A tray made of a half sheet of imported tin. The full sheet was 13 3/4" x 10".

HALLMARK. An identifying mark, proving authenticity.

HAND SCREEN. Miscalled a fan or face screen. Used to ward off heat from the fire.

HEPPLEWHITE, GEORGE (died 1786). English cabinet maker. Lightness and grace distinguished his work. Perhaps not the originator but certainly the most consistent user of the shield back. He favored slight legs: plain, fluted, or reeded, tapering to a spade foot, known as a spider leg. The backs of his chairs were frequently adorned with galleries. He painted and japanned his work, often satinwood, with painted wreaths and festoons, amorini and musical instruments, also floral motifs. He employed the inlay which was so popular in the third quarter of the 18th century.

HEPPLEWHITE PERIOD (1785-1800). The style of furniture named after the London cabinet maker, George Hepplewhite, featured slender, delicate pieces with square,

tapering legs in mahogany, frequently contrasted with
satinwood inlay or veneer. The decoration consisted
of carved drapery festoons, the Prince of Wales feathers
and inlaid overpanels of satinwood in the form of sun-
bursts, spread eagles and conch shell medallions. The
handles were oval, stamped brass plates.

HEX SIGNS. Seen in a few counties only, in Pennsylvania, as painted decorations on barns. A star-like
emblem within a circle, these symbols are thought to
be an early 20th century addition to the magnificent
barns of Pennsylvania, rather than signs to ward off
evil spirits. (Contrary theory to be considered since
"hex" is the German word for witch.) Reproductions
are very popular today far beyond the boundaries of
Pennsylvania.

HIGHBOY. A tall chest of drawers, sometimes on a lowboy type base. Also called a "tallboy."

HITCHCOCK CHAIR, AMERICAN (1820-1850). Named after
Lambert Hitchcock, Connecticut. A chair painted,
grained, stenciled and frequently having gold leaf
units similating the earlier expensive ones, from
which they were derived.

HITCHCOCK STYLE. Adaptations of the original Hitchcock chair during the same period.

HUDSON RIVER SCHOOL OF PAINTING, 19th century. The
earliest school of landscape painting in the United
States, founded by Asher Brown Durand and Thomas Cole
in 1841. Looking glasses and cornice boards are found
with Hudson River Valley scenes, probably inspired by
this school.

IMPASTO. In painting, the application of thick pigment to a surface to give relief, accent or a third di-
mentional look.

INDIA INK (INDIAN INK). A pigment composed of a mixture of lamp black or burnt cork with gelatin and water.

INDIAN WORK. The English decorated, japanned articles with "Indian" or Chinese designs. "Indian" was a 17th century term for anything oriental and was also used to describe the Chinese style of ornamentation in the 18th and 19th centuries. Its use originated when the English were forced by the Dutch -- at that time the proclaimed lords of the sea -- to pick up cargo on the Indian coast where it had been left by oriental vessels.

JAPAN. Black asphaltum varnish for coating metal, papier-mâché and wood in imitation of lacquer, also known as "Brunswick black," "japan black" and "black japan."

JAPANNED. Varnished with japan.

JAPANNER. One who coats the surface with asphaltum varnish. Later it was used in a broader sense in regard to both decoration and manufacture.

JAPANNING. This is an imitation of oriental lacquering, and was developed in the 18th century by European craftsmen. They used a varnish composed of seed lac and spirits of wine in contrast to the sap of the rhus vernicifera, used by the orientals.Pseudo-oriental designs were produced on furniture by means of this varnish, metal leaf or dust, paint or whiting. Furniture thus treated was in vogue from the middle of the 17th to the middle of the 18th century.

JAPAN WARE. The name given to decorated articles imitating the oriental lacquer work imported by the tea traders.

JARDINIÈRE. An ornamental stand or receptacle for flowers.

JOINER. A cabinet maker who may also have done his own decorating.

KAST or KAS. A large cupboard in the Dutch style, usually with a heavy overhanging cornice.

KEYHOLE PIERCING.

KIDNEY-SHAPE. An article in the shape of the human kidney.

KING'S GOTHIC. A subtly-pointed Gothic-shaped tray, sometimes with a sandwich edge or a narrow edge with calligraphy (Chinese characters).

KNOBS. Metal, on coffee or teapots, as made by the Dover Stamping Company.

LACE EDGE. A colloquial term, possibly originating with Mrs. Brazer, to describe the trays with pierced edges which originated in Pontypool, Wales in the latter half of the 18th century.

LACE EDGE PAINTING. See the entry in the chapter on "Design."

LACQUER. A high gloss, hard-to-penetrate finish, achieved by padding up and rubbing down many coats of resinous varnish.

LANCET. An English, pointed Gothic arch.

LAP TRAY. A parlor maid's tray, kidney-shaped, to hold in one's lap.

LATE FLOWER PAINTING. Peasant in style; casual, quick, stylized. Not realistic. Opaque.

LATTICE DESIGN. Open work of parallel lines.

LAVABO. A two-piece tank and wash basin, originally used in monasteries.

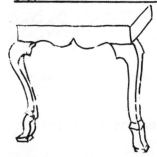

LEGS, CABRIOLE, pied de biche, or
doe's foot. Also sometimes called
"donkey's foot."

LEGS, CABRIOLE, shaped in a double
curve, the upper part swelling out,
the curve swinging in toward the
foot, which again flairs out.

LEGS, SPLAYED, with slight flair at
bottom.

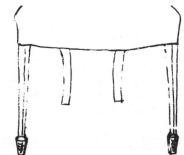

LEGS, SQUARE, tapered, with spade
feet.

LIMN. To paint or draw or illuminate, as books and
manuscripts.

LINER. Painter of borders and rims; a filleter.

LOOKING GLASS. An object having a nearly perfect reflecting surface.

LOWBOY. A table, often a dressing table, with drawers.
Similar to the lower part of a highboy.

LOZENGE. Diamond-shaped. Refers to
piercing on so-called lace edge trays.

LUCIFER. A friction match, drawn between two pieces of
sandpaper to light.

MAHOGANY. Any of the various shades of brownish red
or reddish brown.

MARBLEIZE (MARBLING). To make, stain, grain or vein
in imitation of marble.

MATCH HOLDER. A container without a cover, for holding
matches.

MATCH SAFE. A container with a cover, for holding
matches.

MEANDERING LINE (Usk pattern). Not
necessarily bound by striping. Also
called "narrow crimson." Larger and
less even than stormont.

METAL LEAF. A sheet of metal gold, silver, copper,
aluminum or tin foil. We use the term "metal leaf"
for later and mass produced work, where the leaf is
heavier.

MEZZOTINT. A method of copper-plate engraving.

MIDLANDS. The central counties of England which include
Bilston, Birmingham and Wolverhampton.

MIRROR. A term referring to any polished surface,
either metal or glass, used to reflect objects.

MIRROR KNOBS. Enameled knobs, optionally placed at
the base of the side columns on architectural looking
glasses.

MOLDING. A more or less ornamental strip.

MONEY BALANCES AND WEIGHTS. A tin case which held
weights and balances. Could these have been intended
for gold dust?

MONTEITH. A bowl with notched rim to hold the stems
of wine glasses while the glasses were cooling.

MOTHER-OF-PEARL. See the entry "Pearl shell," page 351.

MOURNING or MEMORIAL PICTURE. The mourning picture was
particularly appealing to the sentimental school girl
at a time when the death rate, especially of children,
was so high. Around the 1800's may be described as it's
high point. It usually included classical figures
weeping over tombs and classical urns, flanked by loved
ones, weeping willows, and landscape features in the
distance.

THE ORPHANS.

Water color mourning picture
Connecticut, circa 1830

MURAL. A wall painting, usually of a scenic nature rather than a stylized design.

NACRE. See the entry, "Pearl shell," page 351.

NEGATIVE STENCILING. The use of a solid cut piece of linen by applying powders around the edges, leaving a silhouette. Sometimes called a "silhouette."

NEO-CLASSIC. Pertaining to the revival of classical tastes and styles in art.

NIGHTSTAND. A stand to hold chamber ware.

NON-ARCHITECTURAL LOOKING GLASS. Not having an overhanging entablature.

NURSING ROCKER. A small low rocking chair used by nursing mothers.

OCTAGONAL. Having eight sides and eight angles.

OCTOFOIL. Having eight equal sides.

OGEE. A molding with an S-shaped profile.

ONE-PIECE STENCIL. A stencil cut all in one piece.

ONE-SHEET WAITER. A tray made of a single sheet of imported tin, 10" x 13 3/4".

OPAQUE. Non-translucent. Impervious to light.

ORIENTAL. Pertaining to the Orient or the East.

ORMOLU. Gilt or bronze metallic material used in decorating furniture.

OVAL-BACK CHAIR. Chair back in the shape of an oval, developed by Hepplewhite.

PAPER WARE. See the following entry.

PAPIER-MÂCHÉ. A compound of paper pulp and sizing
molded into articles which were lacquered or japanned
(trays, boxes, cornices, etc.). In France it was mashed paper. In England it was not mashed but consisted
of layers of paper pressed and molded together, a process invented by Henry Clay in 1772 and called "paper
ware" until Jennens & Bettridge revived the term "papier-mâche" in the mid-19th century.

PARLOR MAID'S TRAY. A kidney-shaped lap tray.

PARTIAL GILT. Partially gilded.

PEARL SHELL or NACRE or MOTHER-OF-PEARL. The irridescent interior lamina or scales of the shells of various
bivalves. The use of pearl shell to decorate lacquer
grounds began as far back as the 8th century, but its
modern usage began in the 17th century in Japan, and it
was used on articles exported to Europe. These articles were such a success that pearl shell decoration
was imitated by the Dutch, English and French. In 1825
a type of pearl shell decoration was invented by George
Sauter and was patented by Jennens & Bettridge of Birmingham. Pearl shell was affixed to the smooth surface
with an adhesive. The two most generally used types of
pearl shell were "aurora," with a greenish hue, and
"nautilus" with a pink hue.

PEDESTAL. A base or support for a column.

PEDIMENT. A broad triangular section above a door,
looking glass, portico, etc.

PENNSYLVANIA GERMAN, or PENNSYLVANIA DUTCH, from
the word "deutsch," meaning German, not Holland Dutch.
A style of painting in bright clear colors, highly
stylized. A folk art form.

PENWORK. Line design drawn in India ink with a quill
pen and fine brushes, found mostly on wood.

PENDENT HANGING or PENDANT, which means "hanging."
Used when referring to cornices as pendent balls or
pendent strings of flowers and leaves.

PIE-CRUST. A furniture term sometimes erroneously used
for a tray shape.

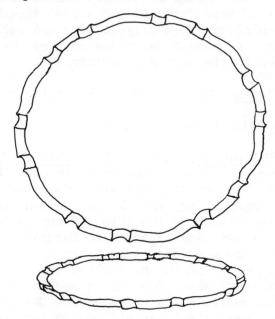

Pie-crust shape, concave, circa 1765

PIER GLASS. A long mirror made of two pieces of glass,
designed to hang between two windows or doors or over
a table.

PIERCED EDGE. A tray edge, die-pierced.

PIERCING. Designs formed by holes cut or punched in
decorative shapes.

PILLAR. See the entry, "Column," above.

PILLEMENT DECORATION. Designs done in the oriental
manner by Jean Pillement.

PILLOW-TOP. Sometimes called "grip top."

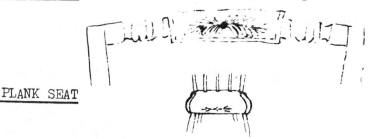

PLANK SEAT

PLATE WARMER. An enclosed cabinet in which dishes are
warmed in front of the fire.

PLATFORM TOP. The raised concave top
on a tin trunk。

PLINTH. The support of the base of a finial; the center
support on which the urn, eagle, etc. is mounted. The
base of a chest which is flush with the floor, and of
some clocks.

POLE SCREEN. An adjustable screen on a pedestal to
shield the face from the heat of a fire.

POLYCHROME. Having many colors.

POONAH. A stencil.

PONTYPOOL. A town in Monmouthshire where japanning on
sheet metal originated; also a generic term for japanned
articles. Presumably the name was transplanted, with
the tinplate, to the Midland tin centers, especially
Wolverhampton, and strengthened by the arrival of the
Welsh craftsmen there. In 1834, four of the Midland
factories still called their products "pontypool," and
to this day the double border freehand bronze rectangular tray is frequently called a "Pontypool" tray.

PRINTED TIN. The lithographic process applied to tin
since 1875 and continuing to the present day. Many decorated commercial containers we see are printed tin.

PUCE. A dark brownish-purple color.

PUNCHED TIN. Embossed design, not cut all the way through.

PURDONIUM. A coal vase (French) with a hinged lid on top.

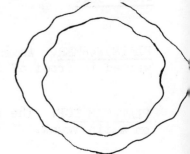

QUEEN ANNE SHAPE. A softly curved oval tray.

QUEEN ANNE VASE SHAPE. Found on chairs.

QUEEN'S GOTHIC. A deeply-curved Gothic-shaped tray, sometimes with a sandwich edge.

RABBIT-EAR CHAIR. See the entry, "Thumb-back chair," below.

RAIL. A slat resting on supports; joining stiles; such as a chair top.

RAKED LEGS. Not vertical but so placed that they slant, the front legs to the sides, the rear legs to the back and sides.

RAW-EDGE. See the entry, "Thin-edge," below.

REDONE. Pertaining to redoing the original design back onto the tray or whatever.

REGENCY PERIOD. 1810-1830, in England.

RENDERING. A translation, version, execution.

RÉPOUSSÉ. Embossing.

REPRODUCTION. That which is reproduced as a copy of
a work of art.

REVERSE PAINTING ON GLASS. The process is reversed,
i.e. the details are done first, the background last.
See the "Reverse painting on glass" entry in the chapter on "Design," also Figs.635-638.

RICK-RACK. A country brush stroke
border.

ROCOCO (ROCAILLE). 18th century French style of ornamentation. Elaborate and profuse designs. Overdone,
florid.

ROLL-BACK SLAT-TOP.

ROLL TOP WITH WINGS. This top slat
indicates the chair was made before
1840.

ROLLED RIM. A tray edge which has been rolled over a
wire.

ROSES AND CASTLES. See the entry, "Bargee art," above.

ROSETTE. A decorative brass rosette applied to a block-
ed corner on non-architectural looking glasses. These
rosettes were of compo, too.

ROUNDEL. An ornament.

RUBBING. A record of an object, produced by rubbing a
lead pencil over a piece of thin paper which is held
over the object to be reproduced, such as piercing or
an indented signature.

CLAY
KING St.
COVIGARDEN

This rubbing came from a round 8" tray and is identical
with that from a snuffers tray.

RUNNER. Sometimes the rocking part of a rocking chair.

RUSH SEAT. Made of rushes inter-
woven, sometimes called "flagg."

SADDLE SEAT. Found on Windsors.

SALEM ROCKER. A Boston-type rocker with the seat
rounded at the back, not rolled at the front, but similar to the Windsor seat. Frequently a yellow chair.

SALVER. A tray on which anything is presented.

SAND SHAKER. Implement used to shake sand over ink on
paper in order to dry the ink.

SANDWICH EDGE. A tray with a horizontal border about
1½" wide.

Sandwich edge of a rectangular tray.

Sandwich edge of a Gothic tray.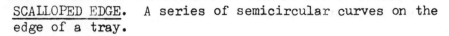

SCALLOPED EDGE. A series of semicircular curves on the
edge of a tray.

SCENIC PAINTING. Found on looking glasses, clocks,
chairs and settees. Scenic stenciling is found mainly
on trays and on some chairs.

SCONCE. A flat-back candle holder to hang on the wall.

SCROLL, ACANTHUS.

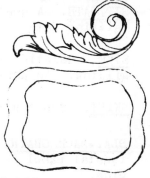

SERPENTINE. Waving or undulating.
Also a tray shape.

SETTEE. A long seat with a back. 1700-1800. The term
"sofa" was used synonymously in English books. In America the term refers to the pieces without upholstery.
The earlier ones looked like two or more chairs placed
together with a single seat. Settees having two chair
backs are called two-chair back settees; if three,
three-back settees, etc.

SHELL. See the entry "Pearl shell," page 351.

SHERATON, THOMAS (1751-1806). Next to Chippendale,
the most famous English furniture designer and cabinet
maker. He published "The Cabinet Maker's and Uphol-
sterer's Drawing Book" in 1791 and by 1802 it had gone
into three editions. This was followed by further publications. He was influenced by Adam and Hepplewhite.
Much of his work was highly ornate and in his final
period bizarre, which ruined British furniture design
temporarily. Swan-neck pediments were characteristic
of his work. He specialized in so-called "harlequin"
furniture, pieces that concealed something, such as a
library table concealing a step ladder; a dressing
table that could serve as a washstand; an ottoman that
had heating urns underneath it, practical in the inclem-
ent English weather.

SIDE CHAIR. A chair without arms.

SIDE POST. See the entry "Stile," page 360.

SIDES. Papier-mâché covers for books, portfolios, blotters.

SITZBATH. A small tub, translated from the German; a "sitting bath."

SIZE. Gelatin dissolved in distilled water. Used in gilding. An adhesive.

SKIRT. See the entry "Apron," above.

SLAT-BACK CHAIR. A chair with a horizontal panel in the back about 5" wide.

SLIP TRAY. See the entry, "Thin edge," page 361.

SMOKED. Similar to marbleizing, using actual smoke on wet paint or varnish.

SNUFF BOX. Small boxes of varying shapes, with a cover or lid, to hold snuff.

SNUFFERS. A scissors-shaped device for trimming candle wicks. Sometimes were called "snoffers," and occurred as early as 1465. Previously known as "candlesheres." Some carried a small box on the under blade. Usually a 6 1/2" to 7" long instrument. The spike projecting beyond the box was for straightening the curling wick before snuffing it.

Snuffers, Usk, Wales, late 1780's. 7" long. Silver-bronzed stormont covered with transparent yellow varnish.

SPICE BOX. A receptacle or group of boxes or tins for storing spices.

SPILL. A twisted paper used to light pipes.

SPINDLES. Slender turnings in chairs.

SPLASHBOARD.   The backboard on a washstand.

SPLAT BACK.   The vertical panel of a chair back.

SPLAYED LEG.   See the entry, "Legs," page 347.

STAMPED-ON.   Design stamped-on article, usually found on thin edge trays.

STAMPED-OUT.   Tin or papier-mâché, formed by pressure rather than molded.

STAR PATTERN.   Popular in Usk (1761).

STENCIL.   A cut-out pattern used in making decorative designs on any surface. A poonah or a theorem.

STENCILING.   The art of applying bronze powders through cut-out patterns onto a tacky varnished surface.   See the entry for "Stenciling" in the chapter on "Design."

STEPPED EDGE.   Similar to a sandwich edge on a tray, only narrower.

STEPPED DOWN.   A type of slat or rail-
ing.

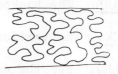

STILE.

STORMONT. A design accredited to Pontypool and Usk. Gold leaf, weaving U-shaped line between stripes. Erroneously called "a meandering line."

STRETCHER. A cross-piece or rung connecting legs of chairs.

STRIPING. A method of framing the ornamentation or enhancing the object with painted or gold leaf line work.

STUMP. A short thick roll of paper or chamois, shaped into a point, used to achieve subtle gradations of light and shade. Used with bronze powders, as in freehand bronze.

STUMP WORK. The technique used in the application of bronze powders. See the entry for "Freehand bronzing," above.

TABERNACLE LOOKING GLASS. See the entry, "Architectural looking glass," above.

TABLATURE. Refers to the picture or painting as seen through a glass tablet.

TABLET. A glass piece in a clock or looking glass, usually decorated. Also the piece of glass used in tinsel pictures, mezzotints, reverse painting and glass pictures.

TALLBOY. See the entry, "Highboy," above.

TALL CLOCK. A grandfather's clock.

c.1800

TEA BOARD. A large 30" to 33" tray with a 3" flange nailed onto its floorboard. A Henry Clay product of papier-mâche.

TEA CADDY. See the entry, "Caddy," above.

TEMPERA. A method of painting in which albumin, gelatin or starch is used as the medium to carry the color.
Water soluble.

THEOREM. Stencils used to create a picture.

THEOREM PAINTING. The art of painting with oils, or
water colors through a stencil onto velvet, silk, or
paper. The most popular subjects were still lifes
with flowers or fruit, and mourning scenes. Reached
the height of its popularity circa 1825. It was a
fashionable pastime for young ladies.

THIN EDGE. Also called "raw edge." Applied to trays
the edge of which was not rolled over wire. These
trays were stamped out. Colloquially called "slip"
trays.

THUMB-BACK CHAIR. A Windsor-type chair with side
posts having a thumb profile. Also called "rabbit-
ear chair" or "common yellow" chair.

THUMBPRINT. Using one's thumb to make a design in wet
paint.

TIN. A low-melting, malleable, ductile, metallic
element nearly approaching silver in color and luster.
When rolled thin it is called tin foil.

TIN TRUNK. A tin box to hold papers, documents, cash,
deeds, trinkets, etc. The size is anywhere from 4" to
19". It has a wire ring or brass handle and a staple
hasp and lock. The top is flat, domed, Gothic, or
platform. Miscalled a "document box."

TIN WARE. All useful or decorative articles made of
tin.

TINPLATE. Thin iron or steel sheets coated with tin.

TINSEL PAINTING. A picture in ink and transparent paint on the back of a piece of glass. The transparent washes are backed with tin foil. The rest of the glass has an opaque background. Also called "crystal painting."

TÔLE. The French word for sheet iron. Should not be used in reference to English or American decorated tinware, which is correctly called "japanned ware."

TÔLE PEINTE. The French term for painted sheet iron.

TORCHERE. A small pedestal candlestand.

TORTOISE-SHELL BACKGROUND. Characteristic of Pontypool. Vermilion red pigment applied in patches on a black japanned ground; two or more coats of brown varnish applied on top, which tones the red to a typical tortoise-shell color. Sometimes crimson varnish was brushed over patches of tin foil. Also found with gold leaf patches.

TRACERY. Very fine gilt design; delicate metal leaf drips.

TRANSFER. To transmit from one thing to another; that which is transferred. Specifically, in art, lithography, etc. A design conveyed by copying ink or by pressure from one surface to another. The finished transfer will be in reverse.

TRANSPARENCIES. A picture made on glass, thin cloth, paper, porcelain, intended to be viewed by the aid of light shining through it.

TRANSPARENT BACKGROUND. Generally asphaltum varnish, more rarely red, yellow, green or blue mixed with varnish, painted over new tin.

TRAY. A kind of flat board with a low rim, made of papier-mâché, tin, iron or other materials, used for carrying or holding articles.

TROMPE L'OEIL. A French term "to cheat the eye"; a decoration giving the effect of three dimensions but being flat. Deceptively real painting.

TURNINGS. Found on stiles, legs and front rungs of chairs, tables, etc.

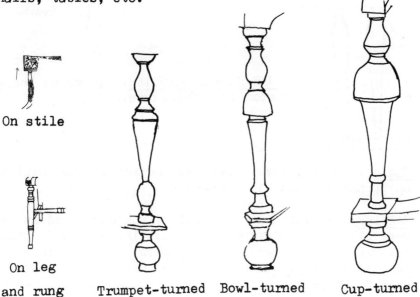

On stile

On leg
and rung   Trumpet-turned   Bowl-turned   Cup-turned

TURTLEBACK CHAIR. A chair with a slat in the shape of a turtle.

TWO-SHEET WAITER. A tray made of two sheets of imported tin, joined in the center. Approximately 13" x 18" in size. Has also been called a "seamed-center" tray.

UNDERPAINTING. See the entry, "Back painting," above.

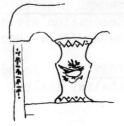

URN-BACK CHAIR. The shape of the
splat gives this chair its name.

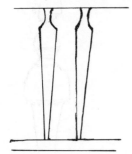

URN-SHAPED BALUSTER. Found on Sher-
aton-type furniture.

USK. A generic term. See explanation in the chapter
on "Tinsmiths and Tin Centers."

VARNISH. A finishing material of gum dissolved in linseed oil, applied with a brush to tin, wood and other
materials for protection. Known to the ancients but
lost to medieval workers who used oil and wax. True
brushing varnish, using dammar or copal in oil, was probably the basis of "Vernis Martin."

VASE-BACK CHAIR. A splat in the shape of a vase gives
this type of chair its name. Miscalled an urn-back or
fiddleback.

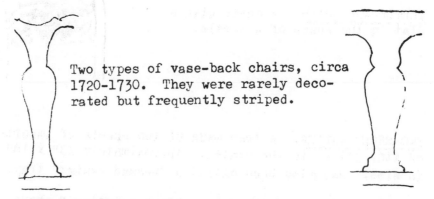

Two types of vase-back chairs, circa
1720-1730. They were rarely decorated but frequently striped.

VERNIS. An old French word for varnish.

VERNIS MARTIN. A generic term derived from a distinguished family of French artists of the 18th century. Applied to a brilliant translucent lacquer used extensively in the decoration of furniture, carriages, small articles, snuffboxes, fans and other things.

VERRIÈRE. See the entry, "Monteith," above.

VICTORIA TRAY. Named after Queen Victoria in 1838.

VICTORIAN PERIOD. The time of Queen Victoria's reign, 1838-1901.

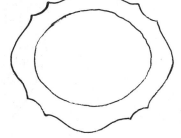

VICTORIAN SHAPE. Point-point-curve shape.

WAFERS. Dry paste in round wafer form to seal letters.

WAG-ON-THE-WALL. A hanging clock without a case.

WAITER. A tray, usually round, up to 18" in diameter or length.

WALL STENCILING. The application of japan oil paint through a stencil onto a dry, not a varnished wall. The same applied to floors gives us the term "floor stenciling."

WATER-CATCH. The lower part of a lavabo.

WET-IN-WET PAINTING. Before one paint is dry another is blended into it.

WHEEL TURNING (at elbow).

WILLIAMSBURG TRAY. A large round tray with a 3" flange.
A modern American tray as made in the 20th century.
Generally decorated with a metal leaf design on a black
ground. So-called perhaps because of its similarity to
the silver salvers of Williamsburg.

Williamsburg tray

ZIG-ZAG GRAINING or TIGER GRAINING. A background found
on tin trunks and other pieces, attributed to Mercy
North. Black paint drawn over an asphaltum backbround
to create a zig-zag pattern. Can be accomplished with
a feather.

INDEX